Ms. Typed

Stop Sabotaging Your Relationships
and Find Dating Success

Michelle R. Callahan, Ph.D.

THREE RIVERS PRESS • NEW YORK

Library of Congress Cataloging-in-Publication Data
Callahan, Michelle R.
    Ms. Typed / Michelle Callahan R.—1st ed.
        p. cm.
    Includes index.
    1. Women—Psychology. 2. Man-woman relationships.
    3. Male selection. 4. Personality assessment. 5. Interpersonal
relations—Psychological aspects. I. Title.
    HQ1206.C235 2009
    646.7'7019—dc22   2008050632

ISBN 978-0-307-40801-3

Printed in the United States of America

DESIGN BY BARBARA STURMAN

10 9 8 7 6 5 4 3 2 1

First Paperback Edition

Ms. Typed is dedicated to the life and
inimitable spirit of my aunt and godmother,
Anjanelle McKinney Carter.

Contents

Introduction

Have you ever caught yourself doing crazy things in a relationship and wondered, What is wrong with me, and why am I acting like this? Have you looked back at how you behaved in a past relationship and asked yourself, Who was that woman, and how did I become her? When riding the relationship roller coaster, sometimes we find ourselves acting out of character and doing things that we aren't proud of. The crazier things get in your relationship, and the longer they stay that way, the greater the likelihood that your unusual behavior will become a habit rather than an exception to the rule. And before you know it, you seem to have become someone new whom you don't recognize and whom you don't want to be but can't seem to get rid of.

Maybe you used to be confident in relationships, but then

you started feeling insecure, and now you need more reassurance that everything is going to be okay. Perhaps you used to date more often, but now you feel you have to dress sexier or have sex sooner than you'd like in order to hold a man's attention. Was dating and being single fun, until one day you couldn't stop worrying about when you are going to meet Mr. Right, get married, and have some kids? Were you once comfortable with your boyfriend hanging out without you, but now you worry about where he is, who he's with, and if he's cheating? In the past were you able to find men who you felt were worthy of your time, but now you feel like you're settling? There are so many ways in which we find ourselves moving away from feeling self-assured and smart in relationships to feeling vulnerable and desperate. Where did this version of you come from? Where is the real you, and how do we get her out on a date?

We all have a dating type or personality that explains how we typically behave in dating relationships. But what if you had so many bad dates and disappointing relationships that it started to have a lasting effect on you? And instead of being the vibrant person you are meant to be, you've become jaded, cynical, jealous, fearful, desperate, resentful, or distrustful. When those changes start to affect your personality, you become Ms. Typed.

Ms. Typed is a woman who has taken on behaviors and personality traits that don't reflect who she wants or is destined to be. When it comes to dating, she is believed to have a less-than-desirable dating personality, but that personality isn't the real her. It's just who she has allowed herself to become as a result of her negative experiences and circumstances. Because she is behaving out of character, she gets mistyped, both in her own mind and by the men she dates. Both she and her dates think she's someone else, because her real dating personality is hidden deep inside, and her true greatness doesn't always shine through.

We all go through experiences that shape who we are, and sometimes as a result of those experiences, we develop negative or counterproductive thoughts and behaviors that sabotage our love lives. Instead of eventually getting ourselves back on track, we sometimes have dating experiences that are dominated by that negativity, and our real personalities get lost. We start to believe that we are that "other" person, and our dates meet Ms. Typed instead of that awesome person stuck living in her shadow.

It isn't your destiny to be a drama queen, a booty call, a mistress, or a stalker, but under certain circumstances you may have allowed yourself to become one or all of them. As a result, you may have lost sight of your true self, which caused you to behave in ways that are out of character for you. The longer you acted that way the more it became a regular part of your behavior and personality, and before you knew it you started acting like someone else. But what if you were mistyped? What if, instead of finding your way back to your old confident self, you stayed out of character? If you are Ms. Typed, you have taken on a dating personality that is probably more of a coping mechanism than a choice.

If you can't seem to figure out why you are always having problems with the men you're dating, consider the possibility that you've been mistyped and you're bringing a lot of counterproductive behaviors to your dating experiences that you

3

need to let go of. When you mistype yourself and take on a personality that isn't who you really are, you cause men to mistype you as well. So if the man you are dating doesn't even know the real you, and he only knows you as Ms. Typed, then it's no small wonder that your love life might not be working out! If you aren't being your best self, then men aren't meeting and dating your best self. They may be dating an angry, prudish, or judgmental you. Your past relationships may not have worked out because the man you were dating didn't get along with the woman you were pretending to be, but he might love the real you if he could ever get to meet her!

When you've been mistyped, every man you date seems like Mr. Wrong. He's married, he's got a girlfriend, he's a workaholic, he's a deadbeat, he's a player, he's a mama's boy. You keep running into the same type of man or the same situation over and over again because you've taken on a counterproductive dating personality that attracts that type. Your dating personality, or dating type, affects what type of men you attract and are attracted to. So when you keep having that same drama over and over again but with different men, you need to look at your own behavior to understand how the things you say and do may be undermining your relationships.

When you wonder why Mr. Wrong seems to be after you, you should look at your dating type to figure out what you're doing to reel him in. If you've been mistyped, and you want to change the way you are acting in relationships, it's even more important for you to understand your dating type. Men also have dating types. There are certain types of men whom you attract and certain types of men who are attracted to you.

Knowing your dating type will help explain what you do to attract different types of men, and what you do that keeps you from being a man's preferred type. Some men don't even know what type of woman they want to date, but they can definitely tell you what type they don't want, and sometimes—even though you don't mean to, but because you've been mistyped—you act more like the type of woman he's trying to avoid. If you or the men you date have mistyped you, then this is your opportunity to find your way back to the woman you are destined to be. Discovering your real dating personality will help you figure out who you are, what you want, and what you need to do to get it. Once you know that, you can choose to become whatever type of woman you want to be.

If you know in your heart that you are one type of woman, but you somehow feel stuck acting like the wrong type of woman, I am here to help you find your way back to your true dating personality. *Ms. Typed* gives you the opportunity to discover your current dating type and understand how different the real you may be from the way you have been behaving. I will explain how your experiences may have driven you toward some of your unhealthy behaviors and created a counterproductive dating personality that has prevented your success in dating. This book provides the tools you need to transform yourself into the type of woman you want to be, and therefore discover your true dating personality. When you think about the dating mistakes you've made in the past, you might believe that those mistakes represent who you really are, but I'm here to tell you that you are probably just Ms. Typed. I wrote *Ms. Typed* to help you get that load of negative experiences

5

and memories off your back, and out of your head and heart, so that you can finally be free of your difficult past to pursue an exciting romantic future.

Why Do You Need This Book?

You know in your heart that you've probably been Ms. Typed in some of your relationships, and it's time for a change. You need to reconnect with the real you. If you aren't currently dating, you may be asking yourself, Why am I still single? Why do I always attract the wrong type of person? Why don't men return my phone calls? Why do my relationships end after we have sex, or only exist to provide sex? This book will help you understand yourself and your past relationships, so that you can discover your true dating personality and prevent remaking the mistakes of the past.

It's far too easy to become Ms. Typed. Maybe one day you look in the mirror and remember the old confident you, and you wonder what happened to her. Or you know deep in your heart that you are greater than your circumstances, but you just don't know how to turn your love life around. Maybe a bad breakup or a string of bad relationships has made you feel less and less like the woman you're supposed to be. We all know a woman who is so amazing and has so much potential but somehow always ends up with jerks in dead-end relationships, and we wonder why someone like her would end up with someone like him (or why someone like yourself would end up with someone like your ex). I'll tell you why. It's because she and you are Ms. Typed.

Not only will this book help you rediscover your true self,

but it will also help you create a strong foundation to get your romantic future back on track. If you don't start acting as if you expect to meet Mr. Right right *now*, then how do you expect to be ready for him when he finally shows up? So many women go to bed at night and pray for their "soul mate" or a "good" man to show up in their lives. But what if he showed up and you were so caught up in your past and acting like Ms. Typed that you didn't even recognize that he was "the one"? Under those circumstances, would you really be prepared to put your best foot forward and be in a good mental space to start a relationship? Of course not! Being Ms. Typed makes you vulnerable to dating drama that the real, healthy you would resist. And worst of all, when you are being Ms. Typed, you aren't being yourself. So until you get rid of her, when Mr. Right shows up, that's who he's going to meet!

This book can help you start your personal evolution from Ms. Typed to the true, happier, and healthier you. This way when Mr. Right walks in the door, not only will you recognize him, but with your newfound confidence, health, and inner beauty, you'll have him saying to himself, Now, that's my type of woman!

Why Did I Write This Book?

I have always been fascinated by dating and romantic relationships. As a teenager my friends and I spent hours discussing who did what and why. I couldn't wait to get to college and graduate school to study psychology. I have always been particularly sensitive to the disappointment and pain that women experience as a result of romantic relationships. In graduate school I studied how marriages change over time, how domestic violence physically and mentally impacts married women and their children, and how dating violence affects single women. My doctoral dissertation focused on how teenagers cope with experiences of physical and psychological abuse in their dating relationships and how that abuse affects their psychological well-being. I have always been committed to discovering solutions to women's self-esteem and relationship problems. First, I had to study and understand their experiences, and then I was determined to help them find ways out of these difficult situations. The younger the women were, the more frustrated I was that they had no support or resources. No one tells us how to act in relationships, least of all how to be smart and protect ourselves and by "protecting ourselves," I don't mean acting defensive but just being well informed about how men are, how relationships work, and how sex impacts us physically and emotionally—everything!

Right after I finished my doctoral program at the University of Michigan, I started my postdoctoral fellowship at Yale University's School of Epidemiology and Public Health, working on a research project studying teenage girls at risk for STDs and HIV. The time I spent interviewing these girls helped to change the course of my career and my life. When I interviewed them, I wasn't supposed to be doing anything more than reading off questions and recording their answers. But their pain and their needs were so great that it felt almost impossible to record what they were saying and then ignore it. They wanted to talk to me and I wanted to talk to them, but we weren't supposed to. I resisted as much as I could, but

I knew then that I had to find a way to communicate to women everything I understood about the psychology of relationships. A few years later I started my own relationship and life coaching business, and I started working with the media and providing relationship advice on television. I am always looking for ways to take the research we create in academia and communicate it through the media. For over fifteen years I have studied and worked with women to understand their relationship challenges. I want to help women find ways to cope with their relationship stress and resolve their dating dilemmas.

I decided to write a book about being mistyped because I saw dating types in myself and in the women around me. I have been Ms. Typed, and I was surrounded by other women who were as well, but we had no idea what to do about it. One of the reasons I wrote this book is that I wish it was available to me when I was struggling with feeling like Ms. Typed. I have had my share of dating disappointments. There was a time in my life when I looked back over my dating experiences and felt embarrassed by how often I acted out of character and in ways that didn't represent who I was (or who I thought I should be). I thought I was a "keeper," but I wasn't acting like it! There was the amazing me who I knew I could be, and then there was the "other" me who often showed up for dates. My head kept saying, *You're smarter and stronger than this*, but my body kept acting like it didn't get the memo! I felt trapped in a dating personality that didn't fit who I knew I was supposed to be.

I didn't know it at the time, but I was Ms. Typed. Once I

realized that I needed to change, I decided to take some time away from dating so that I could think things through, give myself some time to heal, and return to the dating world as the real me. So I put myself through the makeover process that I use with my clients, much of which is included here in this book as the Ms. Typed Makeover Kit. Doing these exercises was part of a life makeover for me. Stepping away from dating and focusing on me helped change my entire life. Soon afterward, I quit my job, started my own business, started working in television, and met a wonderful man—and the list goes on!

I have had the pleasure of speaking to countless women about their dating experiences, and I love sharing what I know and understand, as well as helping someone take a necessary next step toward a better life. That's the inspiration for this book. I want to be able to reach all women who want to learn how to coach themselves and improve their dating relationships. Sometimes we don't know what's wrong, and other times we know what the problem is but don't know what to do about it. I hope that this book addresses both issues and leaves you feeling empowered to find the love you deserve.

This book will teach you to recognize your dating type's thoughts and behaviors, things you may not even realize are sabotaging your relationships. Once you start to transform your old thoughts and behaviors, you will break unhealthy dating habits (some as simple as having sex too soon, and some as serious as tolerating lying, cheating, or abuse) and develop new habits (like learning to speak up for yourself and setting boundaries) that promote strong relationships and better represent the real you.

How Do We Get Started?

Since understanding where you've been romantically is the foundation of your work here, you will first take a quiz to discover your current dating type. Once you know your dating type, you can read the chapters written specifically for you. Then use the strategies at the end of each chapter to help you overcome being mistyped and grow. In each chapter you will find:

- A profile of your dating type
- The consequences of being mistyped
- The types of men you attract and the types to avoid
- How you became your type or mistyped
- Advice and strategies for positive change

What's Your Type?

I've discovered through my research and work with clients that most women are mistyped into one or more dating type categories. I will introduce you to several dating types, some or all of which might describe how you have behaved in your relationships in the past. Each type is named in a way to help you remember the dating challenges for that type. You will understand how living out that dating personality affects the type of men you attract or choose, how you handle conflicts in your relationships, and even what you believe or feel about yourself and your relationships. As you read through these chapters, inevitably you may find yourself in one or more of the types. (Many of us fall into more than one category.)

What Are Dating Types?

Psychologists use the terms *personality type* or *type* to categorize and explain the patterns in people's behaviors, thoughts, and feelings in different situations and over time. Recognizing and acknowledging the different patterns among the types reveals people's motivations and shows us how to best support our clients in making desired changes to their lives. These types are often the basis for different types of therapy, coaching, interventions, and general good advice. We use types not only to help us better understand our clients but to help our clients better understand themselves. When you take a closer look at your life, you will see that you behave consistently, even under various circumstances.

Your dating type represents how you typically behave in dating situations. It's like your dating personality. I believe that your dating type describes how you've behaved but not necessarily who you are. Many women have had experiences that led them to be mistyped as something they are not. Bad relationships and difficult life experiences lead women to lose sight of their true character and self-worth. As a result, they react to their circumstances and become mistyped. The dating types will help you understand what counterproductive dating habits you've developed over time and what to do about them.

The dating types described in this book are influenced by research in cognitive, behavioral, and schema therapy, and by research on life and relationship coaching. As psychologists have discovered, some of your habits in dating, and in life in general, are a result of early childhood experiences and long-held beliefs about yourself and the world around you. When it comes to dating, I'm particularly interested in how certain aspects of our personalities, along with our life experiences, shape our thoughts and feelings and cause us to consistently behave a certain way in romantic situations.

Sometimes, even though we change dating partners, we handle dating situations the same way over and over again because of who we have become. We need to be aware of how our habits, tendencies, and preferences are affecting our lives and to learn how to adjust those behaviors or be flexible enough to change them when necessary. What worked in one relationship may not work in another, and because we are such creatures of habit, sometimes we keep on doing the same thing, even when it's obvious that that thing isn't working. Sometimes we don't know what else to do or any other way to handle things besides doing what we've always done. I created these dating types to help you to recognize your dating patterns, to understand why you act the way you do in dating relationships, and to show you how to change those dating behaviors that are no longer working for you or that don't represent who you are.

This book is about the difficulties that women face in dating, particularly when they've been mistyped, so the dating types described here focus on women's counterproductive dating behaviors. There are additional dating types that describe women's healthy personality traits and positive dating behaviors. In this book I am trying to help women discover their true dating personalities that are hidden beneath so many counterproductive dating habits. So I have purposely chosen to focus on the types that represent our relationship problem areas, with the intent to provide helpful and practical solutions.

How You Become Mistyped

No one really teaches you how to have successful relationships or how to date. Instead, you learn as you go, from your successes and your failures. And when you don't learn, you just keep repeating the same mistakes. We're going to stop that process right now. This book will show you that although it takes time, someone who is really struggling in relationships may transform themselves into someone who is very savvy, self-aware, and successful at navigating all relationship challenges.

We develop and grow into certain types of people based partly on our own genetic predispositions and partly on our experiences with our environment. So who we become is a result of our genetic makeup and our interactions with everyone and everything. From your early childhood until now, you observed and were taught things that encouraged and supported the development of your dating type. You learned lessons about relationships from watching your parents, parent-figures, and other family members. You picked up dating tips from your friends, peers, and the men you dated. When you combine that with what you learn from your exposure to television, movies, music, magazines, and books, you can see that there are many forces that influence how you behave in relationships and that can lead you to become Ms. Typed.

Even with all these influences, you get to decide who you are going to be and how you are going to behave. That is true in your life as well as in your relationships. Now a combination of your own natural tendencies, your parents, your dating experiences, and our culture may have led you to become Ms. Typed, but ultimately the kind of woman you want to be today is now up to you. You don't have to be like your mother, your grandmother, your best friend, or the star on the cover of a magazine. In the movie of your life you get to choose what role you want to play and you write your own lines.

Your dating type certainly was made and came from somewhere, but where she came from doesn't dictate where she is going. It is up to you to decide whether your dating type is working for you. If it isn't, because you've been mistyped, you have the strength, wisdom, and power to change from that type into a happier and healthier you. I am going to help you think about your life so that you can remember when and how you became your type or were mistyped. The idea here is not to blame anyone but to show you where these behaviors came from.

You can't control what you experienced as a child, but you can control what you experience now. You don't have to allow anyone to define who you are or what you can accomplish. Your dating type isn't like your blood type—it can change! But until you recognize what you are doing that isn't healthy, you won't change. Recognizing the origins of your dating type will also help you resist becoming mistyped again in the future or looking to those same unhealthy sources for information about relationships. You may discover along the way that as much as you love your best friends, they are terrible at relationships and give awful advice. That doesn't mean you love them any less as friends, but it does mean that you may need to stop asking for and taking dating advice from them.

You may also discover that you have bought into many of Hollywood's relationship fantasies and you are walking through life allowing a fairy tale to mistype you and determine what you expect of yourself and your mate. When you think about it objectively, you might say, "Of course, what we see on TV and in the movies isn't real." But are you sure that you haven't internalized some of the messages and made them part of what you subconsciously believe about relationships?

I want you to jump right in and kick off this process by answering the following questions about your behavior in your past relationships. There are no right or wrong answers, so it doesn't matter which type you are, if you are many types, or if you are all of the types. Without overanalyzing the questions, just quickly read and answer each one. Don't answer based on what you want to be true or wish were true about yourself, just be honest. Once you are finished with the questionnaire, you will score it and determine which dating type or types best describe you.

Dating Types Questionnaire

Place a check (✔) next to any and all of the statements that describe you or your past experiences.

1. Have you settled for being a "friend with benefits" when what you really wanted was a commitment? ☐

2. Have you had sex with a man you were dating sooner than you wanted to because you hoped it would bring you closer together? ☐

3. Are you looking for your "soul mate" and feeling frustrated because you haven't found him yet? ☐

4. Do you love the challenge of chasing down a "bad boy" for a date? ☐

5. Have you become really upset when a man you were dating did something inconsiderate like forget to call you back or cancel a date at the last minute? ☐

6. Have you ever felt more like you were a man's mother than his partner? ☐

7. Have you ever insisted that the man you were dating spend all his time with you, and if he didn't, you got upset? ☐

8. Are you too busy with your career to make time to date? ☐

9. Do you usually try to focus on the good and overlook the bad when it comes to the men you date? ☐

10. Do you think that most men aren't good enough to date you? ☐

Dating Types Questionnaire (continued)

11. Have you ever dated a man who was already in a committed relationship with another woman? ☐

12. Have you had sex with a man on a first date hoping you could guarantee a second date? ☐

13. Is your biological clock's alarm ringing off the hook, and do you wish Mr. Right would show up right now? ☐

14. Does dating "nice guys" bore you? ☐

15. Do you feel like eventually, sooner or later, men always disappoint you or let you down? ☐

16. Do the men you date ever become dependent on you to handle their day-to-day responsibilities for them or solve their problems? ☐

17. Do you constantly call your man and keep track of his whereabouts? ☐

18. Have you hidden behind your work as a way to avoid getting close to someone? ☐

19. When things aren't going well in a relationship, are you usually optimistic that your man will change for the better? ☐

20. Do you or any of the men whom you've dated think that you're a perfectionist? ☐

21. Have you ever had a hard time speaking up or sticking up for yourself in a relationship? ☐

22. Do you think you can control men with sex? ☐

23. Before the relationships ended, did you think each of the men you were dating was "the one"? ☐

24. Do you like it when the man you're dating calls looking for you several times a day, even though you know he's probably just checking up on you? ☐

25. Are you still mad at one of your exes for how he treated you when you were together? ☐

26. Have you spent a lot of your free time doing things for the man you're dating, when you really needed to spend that time doing things for yourself? ☐

27. Have you acted jealous or possessive of the man you're dating? ☐

28. Did an ex-boyfriend ever hurt you so much that you avoided dating for a long time? ☐

29. Do you ever get a gut feeling that something is wrong in your relationship, but you ignore it because you don't want to face the truth? ☐

30. Has it ever been hard for you to date because you or your successes intimidate men? ☐

31. Have you ever been attracted to or dated a man who was always too busy to give you the attention you needed? ☐

32. Do you believe that you can have sex like a man without any emotional strings attached? ☐

33. Is it important to you to always be in a relationship? ☐

34. Have you ever enjoyed competing with another woman for a man's attention? ☐

35. Have you ever dated a man who psychologically or physically mistreated or harmed you? ☐

Dating Types Questionnaire (continued)

36. Have you ever spent more time helping your man take care of his business and meet his goals than you spent taking care of your own? ☐

37. Do you often ask a man you're dating how he feels about you and where your relationship is going? ☐

38. Do you believe that men usually let you down and that they can't really be trusted? ☐

39. Have you ever found yourself making excuses for the inconsiderate or inappropriate behaviors of the men you date? ☐

40. Has it ever been hard for you to just relax and enjoy yourself on a date because you really wanted everything about the date to be perfect? ☐

41. Have you ever found yourself waiting around for the man you're dating to make a commitment? ☐

42. Have you ever continued dating someone who was only interested in sex when what you really wanted was a relationship? ☐

43. Do you think it's better to try to work things out in a rocky relationship than to be single? ☐

44. Are you attracted to the challenge of dating an emotionally unavailable man or a man in a relationship with another woman? ☐

45. Have you overreacted and become too emotional when the man you were dating did something to upset you? ☐

46. Have you ever tried to change things about a man you were dating to make him more attractive to you? ☐

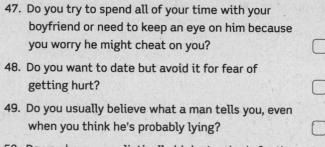

47. Do you try to spend all of your time with your boyfriend or need to keep an eye on him because you worry he might cheat on you? ☐

48. Do you want to date but avoid it for fear of getting hurt? ☐

49. Do you usually believe what a man tells you, even when you think he's probably lying? ☐

50. Do you have unrealistically high standards for the type of men you date? ☐

Scoring

Add your number of checks (✔) for the following questions:

1, 11, 21, 31, and 41. Enter the total here: _____. The higher the number, the more you are like **Ms. Second Place**.

2, 12, 22, 32, and 42. Enter the total here: _____. The higher the number, the more you are like **Ms. Sex Machine**.

3, 13, 23, 33, and 43. Enter the total here: _____. The higher the number, the more you are like **Ms. Soul Mate**.

4, 14, 24, 34, and 44. Enter the total here: _____. The higher the number, the more you are like **Ms. Drama Queen**.

5, 15, 25, 35, and 45. Enter the total here: _____. The higher the number, the more you are like **Ms. Bag Lady**.

6, 16, 26, 36, and 46. Enter the total here: _____. The higher the number, the more you are like **Ms. Mom**.

7, 17, 27, 37, and 47. Enter the total here: _____. The higher the number, the more you are like **Ms. Anaconda**.

8, 18, 28, 38, and 48. Enter the total here: _____. The higher the number, the more you are like **Ms. Independent**.

9, 19, 29, 39, and 49. Enter the total here: _____. The higher the number, the more you are like **Ms. Rose-Colored Glasses**.

10, 20, 30, 40, and 50. Enter the total here: _____. The higher the number, the more you are like **Ms. Perfect**.

How to Interpret Your Score

◆ Your dating types are the types where you placed at least one check next to the questions for that type. The more checks you have, the more that type describes you.

◆ You may find that you have a lot of checks in one or two types and then only one check in others. The type that you have the most checks in is your primary type and probably most accurately describes you. The types where you placed only one check are your secondary types. Your secondary types also describe how you *sometimes* act in relationships, but they may not describe you as well as your primary type.

◆ That you didn't place any checks next to certain types doesn't mean that you don't sometimes act like those types. You can benefit from reading about all the dating types because at some point most of us have faced, or will face, the core challenges of each dating type. Knowing how to cross that bridge before you come to it can save you a lot of trouble in the end.

The Dating Types at a Glance

1. Ms. Second Place

Ms. Second Place allows herself to be put in second place to everything else in her man's life. She may be second to his wife, his career, or his friends. She isn't a priority, she knows it, and she lives with it. She has forgotten what a special person she is, so she thinks she has to settle for second, when she deserves first place.

2. Ms. Sex Machine

Ms. Sex Machine settles for physical and sexual intimacy when what she really wants is a relationship and emotional intimacy. She uses sex as a weapon to manipulate men and get what she wants (except a relationship). She thinks she has to give away her most prized possession to buy a man's love and attention, when all she needs to do is allow her great personality to shine, and men will want to know more.

3. Ms. Soul Mate

Ms. Soul Mate believes that life doesn't exist outside of dating, so she wants every man she dates to be "the one." She doesn't know how to just enjoy dating a man while it lasts and admit when the relationship has no future. One day she will find "the one." She just needs to take her time and wait for a man who is deserving of her love and commitment.

The Dating Types at a Glance (continued)

4. *Ms. Drama Queen* ....

Ms. Drama Queen loves a challenge and likes dating bad boys, unavailable men, and players. She thinks that love is supposed to be a challenge and is constantly pursuing dead-end relationships that result in her being rejected. She believes that she has to do something over the top to win a man's heart, when all she needs to do is be herself.

5. *Ms. Bag Lady* ....

Ms. Bag Lady carries around a load of emotional "baggage" and lets her old emotions adversely affect her new relationships. She lets her unresolved problems from the past ruin her present and future. Because she's been treated so poorly, she doesn't realize how wonderful and deserving of love she truly is.

6. *Ms. Mom* ....

Ms. Mom dates men whose lives are "under construction," and she makes it her responsibility to solve their problems. She doesn't know how to stop mothering a man and let him stand on his own two feet. Instead, she needs to apply that nurturing approach to her own life. He already has a mother. All Mr. Right needs is a friend and partner.

7. *Ms. Anaconda* ....

Ms. Anaconda kills her relationships by wrapping herself around a man until she suffocates him. She smothers a relationship by being too needy, too demanding, and too overbearing. She thinks she has to hold on to a man like her life depends on it because she doesn't realize that she is strong and smart enough to stand on her own.

8. Ms. Independent

Ms. Independent has been burned in love before, so she won't let anyone get close to her for fear of getting hurt again. She would rather be alone than risk rejection. When she realizes that letting her guard down doesn't mean being taken advantage of, she can allow her inner light to shine, and men will flock to it.

9. Ms. Rose-Colored Glasses

Ms. Rose-Colored Glasses won't see the truth about the man she's dating or what's wrong with their relationship. She just keeps on going like nothing is wrong—until she crashes into reality. Her optimism is helpful when applied to other areas of her life. But in love it creates a blind spot that hides the truth that she doesn't realize she is strong enough to face.

10. Ms. Perfect

Ms. Perfect is so caught up in a never-ending cycle of perfection and self-improvement that she has no time for a relationship. She is too uptight to let go and have fun on a date, and she rarely finds a man she thinks is "good enough" for her. When she realizes that she is already everything a man could want, she can finally sit back and start enjoying life.

ONE FINAL WORD

Now let me be clear about something. Although we will often talk about what you do that is upsetting to the man you are dating or that might turn men off, the purpose of this book is to help you learn how to do what is best for *you*. I know that for most women, being in a relationship is very important, and as long as that is one of your priorities, I will help you accomplish that goal. But I want to make sure that you make yourself happy, because some of the same behaviors that undermine a dating relationship can also hurt you in other areas of your life. You can improve your love life but also get out of your own way so that you can live a happier life overall. Remember, the happier and healthier you are, the better your dating partner and relationship are likely to be. When you start looking in the mirror and seeing things you want to change, don't do it for him—do it for you. No matter what happens with him, building a happier you is what's most important.

We often realize that we need to change things about ourselves, but we stop just short of doing something about that realization. If you are ready to finally make some changes in your dating life, I challenge you to not only accept the truth about yourself but to get involved in activities that will help you break those old habits and build some new ones. No matter how bad things may be or have ever been, you have the power within you to change your love life. You can do it by letting go of the old thoughts and behaviors that no longer represent who you are, and by letting the new you, the real you, emerge. This book can be the beginning of a new life for you, one where you pursue your personal and professional dreams. You can use the Ms. Typed Makeover Kit to help you get a fresh start. I wrote this book because I want to be there to encourage and inspire you along the way.

Let's get started!

Ms. Second Place

WHAT SHE LOOKS LIKE

- Feels so eager to please that she allows herself to be put in second place in a man's life. She doesn't realize or understand that the longer she stays in second position, the less likely it is that she will ever move to first.

- Needs to feel liked, included, and accepted, which makes her ideal prey for the man who likes to cheat. She is willing to be a friend with benefits.

- Allows herself to be controlled and won't stand up and demand what she wants and needs. She's unclear about her needs, rights, and expectations, so she doesn't ask for them.

- Lacks faith and confidence in herself and her ability to find a good man.

- Doesn't mean what she says and won't take action to get herself out of this situation. She feels she has no other options so she waits her turn . . . forever.

- Tries to avoid conflict by being too accommodating, which always results in being pushed off of his priority list.

- Refuses to leave the man who puts her in second position because she "loves" him.

- Is in second place to a man's career, his social life, and his other girlfriends.

Ms. Second Place's desire is to be first in her man's life, but instead she finds herself taking second place to his career, friends, wife, or other girlfriends, alcohol/drugs, and anything else he values more than her. She puts her needs second, instead of standing up for herself. Ms. Second Place tolerates this treatment due to her need to be liked, her feelings of low self-worth, or her low expectations. She doesn't realize it, but she undermines her chance to be first by her subconscious belief that she deserves what she's getting and by her willingness to settle for it. If she believed she should be a priority and insisted on it, she would only date men who agree with her. She blames the men for treating her unfairly, when she has the ability to influence the situation. When she pretends she is low maintenance and doesn't need much (which isn't true), she sends an inaccurate message that it's okay to put her second. She is afraid to stand up for herself and ask for what she wants. She isn't a priority, she knows it, and she lives with it.

THE ROLES SHE PLAYS

There are several roles that Ms. Second Place plays in relationships, including:

♦ **Ms. Second Place to His Other Girlfriends.** Whether he tells her so directly or not, she is a friend with benefits or a booty call. He has many girlfriends, and sex rules his life. She is determined to hang on in hopes that she will move up the ranks to number one, but in the meantime she is just one of many. She settles for what she can get rather than having nothing at all. She doesn't realize that she may not even take second place, she might be in tenth. All she knows is that she wants the same thing that all of his other women want—him.

♦ **Ms. Second Place to His Social Life.** Her man is the life of the party, and she makes a good nurse for his hangovers. There is always an event he needs to attend or drinks with friends that leave her home alone. Spending time with others always gets the prime time slot on his calendar, and she gets stuck with the leftovers after hours. She can't compete with his desire to party. But she likes to date him because he's the kind of guy everyone likes, he has lots of friends, and he is a lot of fun. She trades her space on his priority list for the chance to spend any time with him.

◆ **Ms. Second Place to His Career.** She is in love with a workaholic who takes calls over dinner, on vacation, and even during sex. There is no time that's reserved just for the two of them. It seems that whenever she wants to talk about their relationship or needs more attention, work is his excuse for why he can't be there for her or to take the relationship to the next level. She's attracted to his money and power, so she is willing to settle for second place as long as he keeps paying the bills and they keep living the good life.

Just Like You ....

Who else is like Ms. Second Place? Ms. Second Place often has some of the same dating challenges as Ms. Bag Lady. Both of you struggle with taking control of your lives and relationships. So be sure to read about Ms. Bag Lady as well. And like Ms. Mom, Ms. Second Place feels an obligation to put her own needs second to those of a man, so visit the chapter on Ms. Mom. Lastly, being in second place can put you in some dramatic situations, so check out Ms. Drama Queen too.

JESSICA'S STORY

Richard promised he was going to tell his wife he wanted a divorce by the end of the week. His girlfriend Jessica couldn't wait for them to finally be together. All the sneaking around was beginning to take its toll on her. Of course, she enjoyed accompanying him on all his business trips. They traveled first class, staying in the best hotels and eating at the best restaurants. In those moments she felt like she was his wife, meeting his clients and colleagues, and clutching his arm at the finest social events. But when they were home, she spent most nights eating dinner alone and waiting for the phone to ring. His wife had recently discovered his mysterious extra cell phone (he had two already), so Jessica could no longer call him whenever she liked.

Sometimes he would sneak by for a twenty-minute quickie. She was glad to see him for any length of time, but she often cried afterward—lonely, missing him, and feeling a little bit used. But recently she had been more optimistic. She and Richard were apartment shopping. They finally decided on the place they would share just as soon as he told his wife it was over and he moved out. He was coming to sign the lease agreement, and Jessica couldn't have been more thrilled. She greeted him at her door in new lingerie with a big smile, a pen, and the agreement in hand. But her face fell when Richard said he had bad news. His wife was pregnant. He was still planning to leave her, but of course he couldn't leave right now—he needed to find the right time to tell her. The new apartment would have to wait awhile.

So What?

It seems pretty obvious that on some level, despite her occasional happiness, Jessica was very unhappy in this relationship. She was in love with someone else's husband, waiting in second place for him to leave his wife for her. In the meantime she was missing out on most of the benefits that come in a monogamous relationship. She had little, if any, control over when she saw Richard, or for how long. Except when they were out of town, she rarely met him in public, and she spent most of her time alone. She used to be closer to her friends and family, but hardly anyone approved of her year-long relationship with a married father of three kids. So she eventually stopped talking and hanging out with everyone but him. The situation obviously met some of her needs, but overall she was compromising so much that it was hard for her friends and family to support her in this role. Jessica tried to explain what a special connection they had, and how she feared that no one else would love her as much as he did, but they could see the toll this was taking on her, and they believed she could do better.

Jessica was also attracted to Richard because he was financially stable and took her out on dates, bought her nice things, and called her every day. They had intense sex. On the surface that sounds great—until you factor in that he was married. She wanted to date someone who would treat her as Richard did, except for his emotional and practical unavailability. She was willing to settle for what she could get, turning a blind eye to what she couldn't. She thought she wanted to be in first place with him, but she should watch out for men like Richard who enjoy having two women. Even if she became first in his life (and no one else but Richard ever really was first), someone else would probably be there as Ms. Second Place!

It wasn't Jessica's destiny to be Richard's mistress—she was mistyped. Intellectually, she thought she should be able to do better, but emotionally she lost her confidence in her ability to find the right man for her, so she settled for much less.

When you are in second place, you miss out on opportunities to date someone willing to put you first. Instead of waiting for that man, you settle for Mr. Right Now. If you date a man who makes it clear that you are not a priority, and then you agree with him, you can't really expect him to change his position. If you wanted to be first, then why would you accept anything else?

You have to say yes to what you want and no to what you don't. Make it clear to the men around you. You set the tone. You let men know what will or won't fly in a relationship. When you agree to be a mistress or a booty call, you are sending the message that it is acceptable to you. Many men will happily agree with you.

You are writing and directing the film that is your life, so you get to decide what happens next. If you don't want to be in second place, you have to say and do things that make that clear to the men around you. Turn down a booty call, and tell him to call you at a decent hour next time. Don't put yourself in a situation where you could start to fall for a married man or a man who already has a girlfriend. Your happiness is at stake, so you have to think ahead and consider how men are going to interpret your behavior. Whatever you say or do is going to tell them what approach to take with you. If you want them to approach you like you are important, then you have to think and act like you are. Period.

I want to address another issue that affected Jessica and Richard's relationship. As I mentioned before, over time Jessica became separated and isolated from her friends and family. They weren't happy about her having an affair, but they still loved her and wanted to be a part of her life. Richard knew however, that they all disapproved of him, so every chance he got, he made attempts to discourage Jessica from talking to or spending time with them. He was afraid that they would eventually convince her to leave him. As long as Richard could keep Jessica away from anyone who disapproved of their relationship, he could continue to keep her on a string and keep having his cake and eating it too.

Many men try to control women by isolating them from their friends and loved ones. They convince women to slowly disengage and disconnect from the people and organizations (work, school, church) that might give them the resources to break away. This is all usually very subtle and comes in the form of very logical explanations of what's wrong with these people and groups. Before you know it, his arguments make so much sense that you have no friends, no hobbies, and nowhere to go. Ms. Second Place is tolerating a situation that isn't ideal or healthy for her, and chances are that the less support she has outside her relationship, the less likely she is either to stand up for herself in the relationship or end it. If she stays connected to friends and family, it's more likely she will have the confidence and support to leave a bad situation.

Why It Matters

So other than the above, what are the negative consequences when you allow yourself to be in second place in a man's life?

♦ **You experience low self-esteem and a lack of confidence.** The longer you remain in a situation where you are being treated as unimportant, the greater the likelihood that you will internalize that experience and convince yourself that you are unworthy of being treated properly. Feeling unworthy of love, respect, and consideration can lead or contribute to low self-esteem. Low self-esteem and low self-worth cause you to lose your confidence. When that happens, you aren't strong enough to ask for what you want in a relationship. This will create a cycle that leads to you continuing to build relationships in which you again find yourself second.

◆ **You lower your expectations, have fewer boundaries, and become more accommodating.** The lower your confidence and self-esteem, the lower your expectations for the man you are dating. After being in several "second place" relationships, you lower the bar so much that you no longer expect to be put first. With lower expectations come fewer boundaries. Over time you become more accommodating and agree to tolerate more and more unacceptable behavior. You may even start to seek out this kind of man because he is what you are used to and you've accepted this role and position in your dating relationships.

◆ **You have unmet needs.** Allowing yourself to be treated this way means accepting that your emotional, physical, sexual, and practical needs are not going to be met. You are essentially telling men that you accept whatever they are willing to give, as opposed to insisting and demanding that your needs be met in some, if not all of these areas.

◆ **You are unhappy.** No matter how you slice it, no one truly enjoys being treated like they are second to anyone or anything. You have survived at least one relationship like this, but if you examine it carefully, you will discover that you didn't experience the happiness you'd like. Or you may not even expect dating to bring happy times. But it should. Coming in second could be robbing you of the happiness, fun, and pleasure you deserve.

◆ **You become angry and resentful.** Being undervalued and missing out on what you need in a relationship can make you very angry. You resent feeling stuck in a one-sided relationship and are angry with yourself for not standing up for what you want and need.

JUST HER TYPE

If you are Ms. Second Place, given your tendency to be a people pleaser and an avoider of conflict, you are attracted to men who like to be the center of your attention. Keeping this in mind, you need to be very aware of your vulnerability to these types:

Mr. Unhappily Married. Ms. Second Place is Mr. Unhappily Married's ideal playmate. Married men are looking for a woman like you. Of course, all women want to be liked and accepted, but they aren't all willing to do it at the cost of their own needs. Married men can't put you first—they already have one person, if not more, in line ahead of you. They prey on your secret desire to be in first place. They will forever promise to someday make you first, but they won't **because you have already agreed to be second**. Your best strategy:

avoid them like the plague because any relationship with a married man is a dead end.

Mr. Player. This man loves women and lots of them. You can't even be guaranteed second place in his life. Once you figure out he's a player, you date him at your own risk. Because he likes to date a lot of women at the same time, you can neither reach him when you need to talk, nor see him except after hours. It may feel fun and challenging in the beginning, but eventually you will feel used and frustrated. You know that you aren't a priority in his life and that if you aren't willing to play his "one of many" game, then he will simply find someone else to replace you.

Mr. Money. Mr. Money is a power player. Professional success and financial reward rule his world, and relationships come second. This means that when you are with him, whatever he can do to move his career ahead and make more money will always be his first priority. His long hours mean that he rarely has time to sit, listen, or pay attention to you. You usually get to see him only briefly and only when it is convenient for him. He tries to make up for it with expensive gifts, but if you want more than designer handbags, he may not be able to provide it for you.

Mr. Needy. When you and Mr. Needy take a look at his life, you both agree that he needs more help than you do, so both of you tend to spend more of your time and collective resources meeting his needs than yours. That puts you right back into second place again. You are vulnerable to him because he will make you feel guilty for getting what you want when his wants seem so much greater. Then you yield to his needs, and you never find the time or the circumstances to meet yours.

Mr. Addict. When you are dating someone with an addiction, you will always be second place in his life. He is so busy struggling to keep up with his addictions and bad habits, you become an enabler to his addictions or someone who helps him pick up the pieces when things fall apart. As long as he has this illness, he will choose to be with his alcohol, drugs, women, gambling, or whatever it is that he allows to rule his life. He doesn't have the emotional or practical space to take care of you and your needs. How can he? He can't even care for himself properly.

How You Became Mistyped as
Ms. Second Place

So, how did you become Ms. Second Place? You probably learned from many different sources that your needs came second to those of others, whether those other people were your boyfriends, parents, siblings, or friends. Here are some examples of experiences that could have led to you coming in second:

- The men you've dated may have tried to convince you that you should go along with whatever they wanted, otherwise they wouldn't date you.

- You were taught that a man's needs should come before your own.
- You watched your mother or other women around you putting themselves in second place in their romantic relationships.
- While your parents were busily absorbed in their own issues, you may have been left in a caretaking role—for yourself and/or the rest of your family.
- Growing up, you may have not been a priority in your parents' lives, and you may have learned through that experience that you and your needs were not important.

Now that you understand how you may have become mistyped as Ms. Second Place, you can change the parts of her that have a negative impact on you and your life.

A Ms. Typed Makeover: From Ms. Second Place to Ms. Second to None

You need to discover the reasons why you allow yourself and your needs to be compromised and placed at a lower priority than they should be within a dating relationship. Maybe you are so used to being accommodating that you didn't realize that you were fading into the background. And now you don't know how to stop. In addition to discovering why you choose these relationships, you have to recognize the specific behaviors and decisions you make that slowly push you down this path. (See the Ms. Typed Makeover Kit for more information.)

To maximize your happiness and relationship success, you have to stop pursuing one-sided relationships and date someone who wants to make you a priority. The man you are with needs not only to be interested in you and your wishes but also to feel that you deserve to be his number-one priority. You can no longer afford to believe that a man you are dating is more important or more deserving than you. That belief leads you to sit back and accept whatever a man is willing to offer you, no matter how little it is. It won't happen overnight, but it will happen. Here are some suggestions that can help you move there faster.

Insist that your needs are a priority. Going forward, you are going to have to speak up and insist that your needs be addressed. By needs, I mean that you are entitled to be heard and taken care of on all levels. You deserve a say in what restaurant you go to for dinner or what movie you see after dinner. (You may not care either way, but if you do, then that opinion should be considered.) You should have the opportunity to spend time with the man you are dating and be able to reach him by phone or see him in person. Your man should be interested in your life and willing to discuss issues that are affecting you. If you don't want to, you shouldn't have to share your man with other women. The more often you compromise, the more normal those compromises seem and the more compromises you will make.

Suppose you start dating a man who is very nice and is willing to put you first. If you continue to act like Ms. Second Place (not speaking up, acting like you don't have a preference when you do, being fearful of upsetting your date so you defer to his preferences), your dating life will remain un-happy. Ultimately, it's up to you to decide what you want and need, so make sure that your man is aware of what that is, and then insist that your needs get met. If your man is unwilling or unable to meet them, you will have to move on and find someone else who will value you.

Don't be afraid of conflict. Despite how much you hate to argue or be at odds, don't be afraid to stand your ground for what you want, even if it means you argue or ultimately part ways. Women try to win a man over by always letting him have his way. But that will backfire when you train him to expect to get his way every time, which means you won't get your way anytime. You get so used to him running the show that weeks or months into the relationship, you stop speaking on your own behalf and you just go along. You have choices about what you want to do and what kind of relationship you want to have. Don't let him lead you; you can lead him. You usually give up your right to lead and hand it over to the man you're dating assuming that he will do what's right. But you have to teach him what's right for you. When you minimize your needs, they don't get recognized, and they don't get met.

Don't assume that if you give him his way now, eventually he will change his mind and see things your way later. So many women have tried that strategy, and it doesn't work. Here's an example: you lie and say you are cool having a friends-with-benefits relationship, figuring he will eventually like you so much that he will want a committed relationship. You agree to keep dating without a commitment, but he never changes his mind about getting serious. You feel like you sold yourself out, because you granted his wish when you knew it wasn't what you wanted. Be honest about what you want, and if the man you're dating doesn't want the same thing, then you can go your separate ways. You can find a man who wants what you want. Don't be afraid to be honest and take the extra time you need to find Mr. Right.

Clarify and stand by your goals. The man you're dating can't support your wishes and goals if you don't have any, or if he doesn't know what they are. As I've said earlier, to get what you want, you need to spend some time thinking about your goals and purpose. That clarity will cause you to behave in ways that will attract and manifest those goals. If the man you are interested in can't meet your expectations or be supportive and encouraging of your future plans, you need to move on.

Avoid committed and emotionally unavailable men. You are attracted to men who don't really want relationships, although they don't always explicitly tell you that. You're also attracted to men who are unwilling to commit the necessary time to a relationship, or whose definition of one means they are King and you are their servant. Every time you find yourself having to push him for a commitment or you catch yourself complaining that he doesn't act like he really cares about you, those are red flags you need to pay attention to. It's likely that you two are a mismatch. Rid yourself of the fears that lead you to seek out these men. Focus on transforming yourself into a woman who feels confident and deserving of a first-place position.

Say what you mean and mean what you say. Men are good at sniffing out a bluff. The more a man knows about you, the more likely he is to know when you are serious and when you are only trying to act tough. If you want to be first in a man's life, you have to mean it. And you have to be willing to create some consequences for him when you don't get what you need. You have to follow through on those consequences. If you do a lot of talking but you don't mean what you say, he won't feel any pressure to take your demands seriously. If you allow inappropriate behavior to go by unquestioned, you will have no one to blame but yourself. You have to say what you mean and mean what you say. If you don't feel confident enough to do either, then you probably shouldn't be dating right now. Instead, why not work on developing the strength and courage you need to be comfortable enough to ask for what you want? Soon you'll know to walk away when you can't have it.

Be willing to let him go. As long as a man knows that you are so desperate to be with him that you will do anything to keep him, he doesn't ever have to give you what you ask for. As long as you create the impression that it's okay to ignore your needs and wants, things won't change. If you create, however, some consequences (like you will end the relationship), then he knows you mean business. I don't mean to insult men by comparing them to children, but think of it this way: if you tell children to stop doing something and they don't, what do you do next? You introduce a consequence to their bad behavior and explain that if they continue to do something that *you* don't like, they will experience something that *they* won't like. Now, if you just keep asking and they just keep disobeying, and you never introduce the consequence, they won't ever listen to you. You have to be willing to hold them accountable to the change you're requesting. What happens if you always threaten the consequence but never follow through? The children keep disobeying you because they know you aren't serious. Just like kids know how far they can push their parents and what they can get away with, so do men. Start teaching him this early in the relationship before you make any commitments. He needs to know what is expected of him and you need to know what he is capable of before you get too involved emotionally.

Be prepared to walk away. Otherwise, expect to keep getting what you've been getting. If you don't stand up for yourself, no one else will.

Build your confidence. Confidence makes it easier for you to stand up and fearlessly ask for what you want. When you are confident, you trust and know that you can find the type of man you need, one who is willing to work with you. When you lack confidence, you fear being alone and therefore tolerate a lot more from men in the hopes that your relationship won't end.

You can build your confidence by doing things that make you feel good. If there are things in your life that make you feel less worthy, then change them. Maybe you need to further your education, change jobs, or make new friends. If you aren't confident about your appearance, you can work out, get a makeover, or take some style tips from a friend. Whatever it is, start working on it. The better you feel about yourself, the more likely you are to attract someone who feels good about you. And the less likely you are to settle for second place.

Be less accommodating to others in all your relationships. You are not just easygoing and people-pleasing with your man. You are probably also that way with friends, family, and coworkers. You have to start speaking up for yourself and making yourself an equal partner in every arena. Doing it in your nondating relationships will be good practice. It will make it easier for you to assert yourself with men, where you might be more hesitant to push back and stand up for yourself.

With each new relationship, raise your expectations a little higher. I know it is hard to break old habits. I don't expect you to put this book down and immediately be able to transform overnight. It takes time to feel comfortable speaking up and pushing back against other people's agendas. But you can take things one step and one relationship at a time. Don't try to change everything all at once. You can start with your friends and family, with one person. And as you feel more comfortable, change your behavior with others. The same is true for your dating relationships. As you continue to meet and date new men, try to assert yourself a little bit more than you did with the last person.

With each new relationship, ask for more of the things you want until you reach the point where you feel strong and confident that you are being treated fairly and lovingly. As you change, you will attract men and experiences that reflect your new beliefs and feelings.

49

3

Ms. Sex Machine

WHAT SHE LOOKS LIKE

◆ Believes she can have sex like a man, and that it won't have any emotional repercussions.

◆ Uses sex to control and manipulate men instead of developing balanced relationships that include nonsexual aspects.

◆ Settles for physical and sexual intimacy when what she really wants is a relationship and emotional intimacy.

◆ Baits men with sex too soon, and it backfires on her when they only come back for casual sex but never for a relationship.

- Is motivated by the belief that sex equals a relationship or that sex equals intimacy, when in a man's mind sex only equals sex.

- Uses her sex appeal to get what she wants.

- Feels empowered by her understanding that men want sex and that she has what they want.

Ms. Sex Machine goes both ways, no pun intended. On one end of the spectrum, she is very happy to have a purely sexual relationship, so she uses sex to get what she wants from a man and skips the emotional stuff. On the other end, she may want a serious emotionally intimate relationship with a man. But if she has figured out that he doesn't want one, she thinks the only way to keep his attention is to give him what he wants sexually until she can convince him otherwise. Because she uses her sex appeal to draw men in, they think she's only interested in sex, so she attracts the booty call boys instead of the relationship men.

THE ROLES SHE PLAYS

How Ms. Sex Machine uses sex in a relationship depends on her goal. Some women use sex as a path to a relationship, others as a way to wield more control within a relationship, some just to have fun:

• **Ms. Sex for Relationships.** Sometimes she is willing to have sex on the first date, or sooner than she thinks she should, because she hopes the sex will help her move toward a relationship. She does not have a high sex drive; nor is she able to have sex with no strings attached. What she really wants is a relationship, and when she goes out on a date with a man she really likes, her attraction to him and her desire to see him again lead her to believe that the best strategy for keeping this relationship going is to have sex sooner rather than later. She knows it's a risk because it gets things moving fast very soon, but it's a risk she's willing to take if she can score a relationship payoff. She incorrectly thinks that because they happened to have sex, they are now in a relationship. You can't equate a man being interested in *having sex* with you with a man being interested in *you*.

• **Ms. Sex for Control.** Ms. Sex Machine has figured out that she can use sex to bait a man, whether it's to get him to come over to visit or to give her something else she wants or needs. She uses sex as her weapon. Some women recognize their power and purposefully ration out sex in exchange for trips or gifts. Other women don't *want* to use sex to get the attention they desire but feel like they have no choice. They feel they have to be strategic and use sex in whatever ways they can to move their relationship forward. They aren't trying to be manipulative, they may not even realize that they are doing it; they're just trying to survive the dating game and are using sex as a lifeline. Ms. Sex Machine is hoping she can bait him with sex and then switch the relationship from a physical one to an emotional one.

◆ **Ms. Sex for Fun.** Sometimes Ms. Sex Machine simply enjoys having sex on the first date. She loves sex and figures the first date is just as good as any other date, so why wait? Good sex is her number-one priority, and since she doesn't know when the next date is coming, she might as well take advantage. She believes that she can have sex like a man, with no emotional strings and no attachments. Or she knows she can't, but she hasn't had sex in so long that she is willing to suffer the consequences, in exchange for the physical intimacy. Some women start off feeling okay with only having sex and later decide they want to try to pursue a relationship. Even though they have already agreed to only having sex, or they don't really want a relationship, they feel used after the sex.

Just Like You ....
Ms. Sex Machine shares a certain denial about what is going on in her relationships with Ms. Rose-Colored Glasses, and she sometimes has conflicted relationships like Ms. Drama Queen. So be sure to read both of their profiles as well.

SHELLEY'S STORY

Shelley liked Dan a lot. It had been a couple months since she'd been on a date, so she was very hopeful that they could start a relationship. After talking on the phone regularly for two weeks, she felt like she knew him. They just clicked. Their first date felt like their third to her. When he asked her back to his place, she was feeling buzzed from all the wine at dinner and happily welcomed the chance to get closer. In the back of her mind, she hoped that having sex with him on the first date would show him how special he was to her. This was not something she did regularly. He seemed to like her, too, so she thought she would be guaranteed a call the next day and certainly a second date. The sex was good, but the outcome wasn't. He didn't call her the next day or for a whole week. He did call her again, though, around ten o'clock on a weeknight, wanting to know if he could get some more of that good old you know what. Happy to hear from him again and excited to move forward, she let him come over, even though she needed to be up early the next day for work. Hello booty call. Good-bye relationship.

So What?

So what's wrong with Shelley getting her groove on during a first date? It's her life. Why do we care if she wanted to have sex right after dinner? What's wrong is that she'd been mistyped. Her goal wasn't to have a one-night stand—her goal was to find a nice man and get into a relationship. Somewhere along the way she bought into the myth that having sex with a man locks him in. That he's going to want more sex and therefore will have to call her back to get it. On one level, that could be true—if the man wants to have sex again, he knows he can call her for it. But it will be very clear in his mind that he is calling her for sex (though he won't present it that way), not for a date (except as a means to get the sex). She will interpret the call as a date and think "success." So here we are with two people on two totally different pages. Shelley thought she made the right decision if he called for a second date, but she really just set herself up to fail because she wanted a relationship, and all he was calling for was sex. It is totally flawed and rather sad to believe that the only way to get a man to call back or consider a commitment is to buy his attention with sex. Worse is to then hope that he figures out he likes your personality too, so you eventually get promoted from sex buddy to someone he "dates."

Some women aren't looking for a relationship but still enjoy sex. They have it with no strings attached, and they still feel good when it's over. If Shelley had been in that group, then chances are she would have felt okay with herself the next day. She wouldn't have built up negative feelings about it. Shelley was actually a member of the group of women, who deep inside feel that casual sex is wrong but do it as a way to get physically close to a man when they know they can't get emotionally close to him. She was pretending that she could have sex like a man, but she couldn't. Hopefully, she figured out that doing this would actually get in the way of having a relationship with anyone.

Shelley isn't a typical Ms. Sex Machine—this was her first time using this strategy, and she had to learn the hard way that it doesn't usually work. She played the sex card on the first date, and that led Dan to respond to her sexually instead of relationally. She had the power to decide how things would go, but she chose the wrong direction. She thought she was just going with the flow, she wasn't thinking that it would shift gears between her and Dan and send him the wrong message. But that's how it works—and that's what happens when you use sex to relate. If you act like you only care about sex, that's all you're going to get.

If you don't want men to expect sex from you, then you can't put sex at the top of your list of things to do when you first start dating. Dan wasn't interested in Shelley only sexually. But once she put sex before dating, he may have felt that he was following her lead. What was he supposed to say? "Oh no, none for me thanks"? Even a man who has noble intentions about taking his time and dating you can fall for the sex bait. Men are following your lead, so when you lead them down a sex path, they follow you. You could also choose to lead them down a relationship path. And they will either choose to follow or not. Remember, you are in control of what image and what message you convey. He will adjust his behavior and expectations based on what you say and do.

That's where women go wrong. They are trying to accomplish one thing, but they end up with another because they gave the man the wrong impression. You sabotage yourself when you pretend to want or need something else. If you really want a relationship, then you have to put dating first. That's how a man will know what you want.

We simply have to get real about men and sex. Men like sex and will do what they can to get it. When a man expresses a sexual interest in you and you respond, you are offering him what he could get elsewhere. So you have to decide carefully whether that is truly what you want to do. Use this equation to help you think it through: Men like sex, you offer sex, therefore men like you. Now replace "you" with the name of any other woman you know. As long as a woman offers sex, men will like her. Get it? So if capturing a man's attention is your only goal, then sex will achieve it. But if you want something more, then don't offer up sex before you accomplish your primary goal.

Why It Matters

If you have been mistyped as Ms. Sex Machine, what are the negative consequences when these strategies backfire?

- **You lower your self-worth and self-esteem.** If you use sex to hold a man's attention, you are telling him and yourself that you are not worthy of love and attention. The longer you go around believing that about yourself, the more likely you are to continue to make very poor choices in relationships, because you will act as if you have to bribe a man to be with you. For your personal health and happiness and your relationship success, you have to love yourself first. You may have never realized you have low self-esteem, but if you can look at your behavior today and see that you are "giving it away," then you do have some negative feelings about yourself even if only subconsciously.

- **You feel guilt.** Women make a lot of decisions in relationships that they feel guilty about and later regret. Having sex too soon or when you didn't really want to are two good examples of experiences you may later regret. That guilt only leads to judgment and even lower feelings of self-worth. Some women feel they are living a sexually liberated lifestyle—at least until the day they change their minds and regret the decisions they've made. Our society is very harsh on women who have sex often and with many partners. Women look back on that time with a lot of guilt and regret and carry around shame for decisions they felt okay with but later wish they could undo. You have to anticipate the results of your actions well in advance of the inevitable experience of those consequences.

◆ **You have repressed emotions.** Unlike the woman who knows she can't handle sex with no strings attached, you may have built an emotional wall that prevents you from realizing when the sex-only interactions are wearing on you. You deny your emotions. You may be tired of it, and ready to settle down, but will avoid the conflict of trying to change your relationships by refusing to admit your desire for more. For some women, it feels like failure to admit that they are unable or no longer want to have sex like a man. So they keep trying. But you shouldn't mistype yourself. You don't have to pretend to be something you're not—if you do fake this, you'll end up unhappy.

◆ **You sabotage potential relationships.** As long as you keep using sex as bait, you will continue to attract primarily sexual experiences. If you are used to putting the sex first in your relationship, not ever expecting it to grow into something serious, you may be sabotaging your ability to develop a more balanced and serious relationship. Again, the direction a relationship takes is your choice. If you allow sex to define who you are instead of just being something you do, you will have a hard time shifting gears when you are ready to settle down.

THE DOCTOR IS IN

Here is a letter written to my online advice column, Ask Dr. Michelle (www.drmichelle.com), by a woman who has been mistyped as Ms. Sex Machine:

DEAR DR. MICHELLE,

We have been sleeping together for a month and yet we do not have any commitment. I really want him to be my boyfriend, but it seems he doesn't want to. I already told him that I like him, but he thinks I'm just kidding and whenever I open up this topic, he just smiles. Tell me. Help me. Please, I don't want us to just be friends with benefits. It's sad because he always texts me with silly, naughty things about sex. What should I do? I can't understand why men are like that.

Thanks!

DEAR MS. SEX MACHINE,

The only chance you have at this becoming a relation-ship is if you stop having sex with this man. He has made it clear that he doesn't want to be in a relation-ship. Here's how I can tell just based on what you wrote in your e-mail: (1) You don't have any commitment: When a man wants to be your boyfriend, he will let you know. (2) You told him that you want a relationship and he pretended he thinks you're kidding. He knows you're serious, but maybe he figures you aren't very serious if you are wasting your time with someone who so clearly does not want a relationship. (3) When you open the topic he just smiles. He's not saying anything because he knows that if he tells you he only wants sex, you might stop having sex with him. And (4) he texts you with silly, naughty things about sex. This is a clear indication of what's on his mind and how he wants to spend his time with you.

I know this isn't the answer you want to hear, but if you want a real relationship, this isn't the man for you, and you should probably walk away before you get any more attached to him. He won't commit to you as long as you settle for having a purely sexual relationship instead. Men don't respect talk; they understand and respect action. He is getting what he wants, so why should he give you more when you will accept less? When you stop having sex with him and insist that it can only be a part of a committed relationship, he will either have to admit he doesn't want a relationship, or he will have to make a commitment. You're wasting your breath, and most importantly wasting your time, if you aren't willing to stand up for what you want. If you want to change direction, get in the driver's seat and make a U-turn. I know it's hard, but you're worth it.

JUST HER TYPE

Given that sex is paramount in your dating relationships, you attract men who put sex first in their lives. In light of your tendency to have sex too soon, or to allow sex to become the glue in your relationships, you have to be very mindful of your vulnerability to the following men:

Mr. Pleasure Principle. Just because you like having sex, and maybe have sex sooner than other women do, doesn't mean that your relationships should only focus on sex. That's why you have to watch out when dating Mr. Pleasure Principle. He is interested only in sexual relationships. As long as you keep dating him, he will keep you locked into a purely sexual role in your relationship.

Mr. Ex Factor. Mr. Ex Factor is the man who will try to slide in under your radar posing as a "nice guy." He is usually an ex-boyfriend or a friend who has somehow become a friend with benefits. He fools you into thinking that he is going to want a relationship, but he conveniently only shows up for the sex. You may think the nerdy friend or the friend from church is definitely a relationship type—but don't make that assumption. Keep your eyes and ears open to discover his true character for yourself.

Mr. Player. Admit it. You like men who are hard to get. Mr. Player can trick you into using your sexuality as a way to try to draw him into your world. Mr. Player likes dating a lot of different women and having sex with you isn't going to change that. Even if he really likes you, he still wants to keep things casual. With him there is no room for advancement from sex to a relationship. How can you stop being Ms. Sex Machine when he is so clear that a relationship is off the table?

How You Became Mistyped as
Ms. Sex Machine

There are so many influences on women that lead them to believe they need to rely on sex in relationships. Here are some experiences that may have influenced you in becoming Ms. Sex Machine:

- Growing up, you may have observed your mother or other women in your family using sex or their sex appeal to get the things they wanted or needed from a man, including attention, affection, money, or protection.
- During your early dating experiences, you probably learned that men have a strong sex drive and that you could maintain their interest by having sex with them (or by pretending that you are interested in having sex with them in the near future).
- You and your friends' earliest dating experiences with boys were sexual. And you grew to expect that sex would be an early and required part of all dating relationships.
- One of your first boyfriends made you feel you needed to have sex in order to keep a boyfriend.
- The men you've dated have been more interested in having sex than being in a relationship.

Girls are dressing in skimpier clothes every day and at younger ages. Condoms and birth control pills give some people the false sense that there are no negative consequences to having sex. So they think, why not? All of these things could have encouraged you to be more sexually active.

A MS. TYPED MAKEOVER:
HOW TO TRANSFORM FROM MS. SEX
MACHINE TO MS. NO MILK FOR FREE

If you are finished being mistyped as Ms. Sex Machine, now is the time to focus on bringing balance to your dating life. The longer you continue to allow yourself to be used sexually in exchange for the illusion of a relationship, the more likely you are to experience low self-esteem, guilt, and pent-up anger. After experiencing several dating relationships like this one, you may start to believe that this kind is normal and that all relationships are like it—at least, all of yours. It is important to transform these negative thoughts and feelings into something more positive so that the next time you are presented with a similar situation, you will make a better choice for your overall health and well-being. Here are some suggestions that can help you move toward your true dating personality:

Wait, and just date. If you want to have a relationship, then date for a while before you start having sex. Don't try to bait a man with sex and then change the rules by expecting a relationship. If a relationship is what you want, show that your interest is in dating, not in hooking up.

Maintain balance in your relationships. Sex may be a big part of your dating relationships, but you don't want it to be the only part or the most significant. You need to pursue relationships with men who have well-rounded personalities and lifestyles so that you will have a balanced relationship and be encouraged to be a more well-rounded person yourself. Your life and relationships need to be about a whole lot more than sex (even if it is your favorite part!). Express an interest in doing other things together (movies, sports, going out to eat) and insist on doing more than staying in and having sex.

Stop having sex with men who don't want a relationship. You have to be honest with yourself when you are dating someone who wants only to have sex. As long as you continue to date that person, whether you think so or not, you are agreeing to settle. Don't bother hanging on thinking that the sex will eventually lead to a relationship. It is a myth that good sex can keep a man. You can catch something, but it won't be his heart. The longer you stick with a man who only wants sex when you want a relationship, the more negative baggage you're going to pick up along the way.

Stop undervaluing yourself. You have to stop selling yourself short by immediately giving away one of the most valuable things you could ever offer someone—your body, and through it an intimate connection to your heart and soul. If you tend to have sex sooner than you think you should, you may need to create a rule or a guideline that says you will wait for at least a minimal amount of time before sex. You may say no sex on the first date or no sex in less than thirty days. Maybe you need to wait for three months. I'm not trying to tell you how long to wait, only that you need to wait. Not only do you need to determine what you want from the man you are considering having sex with, but also you need to know more about him to determine if you should share your body with him. Even if you don't care about being in a relationship and you decide that all you want is the sexual experience, you still have to consider the health implications. Condoms work only if you use them.

And if you have oral sex without them, then you are still exposing yourself to risk for sexually transmitted diseases. This is your one and only body, so treat it like a temple.

Your body is one of the most precious things you have that belongs to you and is controlled only by you. You need to protect it and treat it with respect. Respecting it means not just sharing it with any and everyone, given the potential damage that does to you emotionally and physically. My concern first and foremost is for you. However, I know that you are also concerned with what men want, so let me give you some advice about men. Men are hunters. If you just lie flat on your back, they're going to run past you after someone else who is going to at least make the chase interesting. Got it?

Change the topic. Sometimes a man's idea of foreplay is to talk dirty to you. Not only is he getting his rocks off, but he is also testing you to see how far you are likely to go and how soon you are willing to go there. If you want to keep things from becoming all about sex, then you need to leave a little bit more up to his imagination. Change the topic and see what else this man has to talk about. If all he wants to discuss with you is sex, then you probably don't want to have sex with him or date him—he has only one thing on his mind. Use the conversation as a test, and if all he does is talk about sex, move on.

Don't confuse sex with love. Unlike women, men don't usually get emotionally attached after having sex. Women falsely believe, however, that men are like women. They think that men's interest in sex means they are also interested in the woman. The two things may have nothing to do with each other. For most men, those two things are unrelated. It doesn't make sense to women because they usually wouldn't have sex with a man unless they really liked him or wanted a relationship with him. But most men don't need that deeper interest—all they need is sexual attraction.

Here's an example. A man goes over to his girlfriend's house to break up with her, but before he does, they have sex. He knew all along that afterward he was going to end the relationship, but she had no idea. When he breaks the news that the relationship is over, she is totally distraught but also utterly confused and angry because they just had sex. He leaves, glad that he took his last opportunity to have sex with her. She is beyond confused because she believes that he must still have feelings for her or he wouldn't have just had sex with her. As you can see, just because he no longer likes her as his girlfriend doesn't mean he won't gladly take some sex on his way out the door.

Has your boyfriend ever come over, the two of you have sex, and then unfortunately you get into an argument and he leaves? Some men admit to picking fights when they want to get away from a woman. They may want sex but not want to hang around afterward, so they pick a fight so they can go out with their friends or do something else. Be clear that sex doesn't mean to men what it means to you. Having a hot passionate sex life doesn't mean he is falling in love, that you are his girlfriend, or that he wants you to become his girlfriend.

Talk to your male friends about sex and relationships. If you are surprised by the two examples I just gave you of ways men go about getting sex, then you need to spend some more time talking to men. You need some objective male friends or family members who can tell you the truth about what men think and what motivates them. Ask them how they feel about sex on the first date, how sex is related to commitment, and any other thing you can think of to help give you the low-down on men and sex. The men you are dating won't tell you the truth because they don't want you to hold their indiscretions against them. Find the most honest men you know, who are more interested in helping you than worrying about keeping man secrets, and ask away!

Make sex only one of many things you do well. You became mistyped as Ms. Sex Machine because you gave sex a bigger role in your life than it deserves. You rely on it too often as a strategy to get what you want. You need more than one power play to be successful in relationships or in life overall. Get rid of the belief that your best and most powerful asset is your sexuality, and evolve into a woman who is confident in everything she brings to the table. Instead of investing so much time and energy in all things sex (think of the effort you put into your behavior, looks and environment in preparation for sex), diversify your interests. Try different hobbies, make new friends, and do anything to change your life that can help you broaden your horizons and achieve different life goals. If you focus most of your attention on dating and don't really have any life goals or aspirations, then you need to get some. (See the Ms. Typed Makeover Kit for more information.) Find your passion and know all of your strengths—you have more going for you than what's going on in your bedroom.

4

Ms. Soul Mate

WHAT SHE LOOKS LIKE

◆ Is desperately seeking "the one." She has a similar determination to get married and have children.

◆ Hopes each man she meets is her soul mate.

◆ Feels ready to settle down and can't always distinguish between her driving desire for commitment and her true feelings for the man she's currently dating.

◆ Is determined to be in a relationship at all times and will settle for whoever will take her. In her mind, being with anyone is better than being single.

◆ Has many other names, including Ms. Serial Dater, Ms. Deal Maker, Ms. Desperate, and Ms. Girlfriend.

Ms. Soul Mate believes her purpose in life is to be in a relationship. She sees every man she dates as a potential soul mate, instead of enjoying dating and being selective about with whom she pursues a relationship. She believes that life doesn't exist outside of dating. She wants every man she dates to be "the one" so she can finally stop looking. Ms. Soul Mate always wants to tie a man down and insists on a relationship or commitment. She tries to take every relationship to the next level, even if she has to drag the man kicking and screaming. Because she has difficulty finding someone new, she often believes that one of her ex-boyfriends must be her soul mate. Then she spends all of her time trying to find her way back into an old relationship that is over for good, even if she doesn't know it. If dating is like the stock market, her stock price is way too low, simply because she's always so desperate to sell herself short.

The Roles She Plays

There are several Ms. Soul Mate roles that women play in relationships, including:

◆ **Ms. Desperate.** She is so desperate to settle down that she wants to believe each man is her soul mate, so she can stop looking for him.

◆ **Ms. Girlfriend.** She always rushes commitment and tries to talk the man she's dating into being her boyfriend too soon.

◆ **Ms. Serial Dater.** She's so busy looking for her soul mate that she goes from one man to the next. She looks for a new man before ending her relationship with the old one—she keeps the search going.

◆ **Ms. Deal Maker.** She is constantly looking for ways to close the deal on a commitment. She tries to get her man to commit to a timeline for marriage or children, instead of waiting for it to happen naturally.

Just Like You ....

Who else is like Ms. Soul Mate? Ms. Soul Mate has a lot in common with Ms. Rose-Colored Glasses and Ms. Anaconda. Sometimes her search for "the one" causes her to see and hear what she wants so that she can stop looking. If it seems as if her soul mate is trying to slip away, she won't hesitate to put the squeeze on him to keep the relationship going. So if you're Ms. Soul Mate, be sure to read about Ms. Rose-Colored Glasses and Ms. Anaconda for more insight into how you can change your life and relationships.

KIM'S STORY

After a month of dating, Kim hit Michael with the "relationship talk" over dinner. She wanted to know how he felt about her and where he saw the relationship going. She told him she thought they really clicked, that they had so much in common, and that their relationship had marriage potential. In her mind, telling him this was a compliment, but inside his head sirens were going off. He couldn't believe she actually spoke the word "marriage." *Is she crazy?* he wondered.

Michael agreed that the past month had been great, and prior to that conversation he had every intention of continuing to date Kim. Her insistence on knowing where things were going seemed premature, however, and Michael felt like he was being forced into a committed relationship, when in his mind they still had a lot of dating left to do. He immediately lost his appetite for dinner and for Kim. At first he had thought she was cool, but now he just didn't want to be bothered.

So What?

So was Michael a jerk for letting go of a great woman, and was Kim better off without him? Or did Kim push too hard too soon? Didn't Kim have a right to put her cards on the table? Shouldn't she have made it clear what she wanted so she didn't waste her time?

Like many Ms. Soul Mates, Kim moved too fast. She was already way too invested in Michael and believed that he was the one for her. But she needed to come to terms with the fact that she went through this same process with every man when they hit the one-month mark. She wanted to be married with children. There's nothing wrong with that. But if that was her goal, she needed to spend more time getting to know a man so that she was sure she wasn't desperately trying to snag the first man willing to take the plunge. She was so quick to want to get hitched that she made each man "the one" before she had time to see his flaws and determine their real long-term compatibility. She needed to give relationships enough time to come out of the honeymoon period of the first weeks and months, to see how they handled disagreements, and to discover who he really was before she professed her undying love.

It's good that Kim was clear in her mind about what she wanted. She was much more likely to find the type of man who wanted to settle down if she was honest with herself and clear about what she needed. She still had to approach the dating process a bit more slowly, though, even if she was on the right path with the right person. She had to pace herself. She shouldn't have run ahead of the relationship, dragging her man kicking and screaming from behind!

Telling this story from Michael's perspective makes it a little easier to see why her aggressive strategy didn't work. She simply had no idea that he wasn't on the same page as she was. Her life revolved around him and her dreams of their future together. She incorrectly assumed that the same was true for him.

Why It Matters

When you are mistyped as Ms. Soul Mate, what are the negative consequences of believing every man you date is "the one"?

♦ **You miss out on the rest of what life has to offer.** You may be getting lost in your role as a girlfriend and neglect your other roles, as well as the rest of your life. Having a full and happy life outside of your relationship is what attracts men to you. You will be happier, healthier, and more attractive if you spend time doing more than plotting how to find a husband. You need to find out how to enjoy your life whether you marry or not.

◆ **You sell yourself short.** When your goal is to find your soul mate, but you become impatient with the process, you often end up compromising on your desire to find "the one" and you end up settling for "anyone." Take your time in dating relationships, or you will end up cutting corners. Be willing to see the man you're dating for who he really is. If he isn't the right one, then be willing to continue dating different people, even if that means being alone sometimes. If you are patient, you will get the man you deserve, not just the first man willing to settle down with you.

◆ **You feel disappointed.** If you settle for the first man willing to make a commitment, you may ultimately feel disappointed within the relationship. Sometimes it isn't until after we've rushed into a relationship that we are able to look back and realize that we were lonely or bored and that we settled down too soon just so we could be with someone. If you really want to find "the one," you have to wait for him.

◆ **You perpetuate your fear of being alone.** The more you allow your life to revolve around finding a soul mate, the more you convince yourself you need one. You have to become comfortable with being single and spending time alone. You need to develop enough of a life that you see a man as the cherry on top of your sundae instead of the entire dessert. As long as you remain solely focused on being in a relationship, you will remain in fear of being alone.

JUST HER TYPE

If you are Ms. Soul Mate, given your fixation on settling down, you generally attract men who are willing to commit, but you are also most vulnerable to certain types who you think you can convince to commit and settle down fast. So be aware of your vulnerability to the following men:

Mr. Ex Factor. You are the most vulnerable to Mr. Ex Factor because the more relationships you have that didn't work out, the more convinced you become that one of your ex-boyfriends must be your soul mate. You two may have been first loves. Sometimes your memory of the good times blocks out your memory of the bad. Chances are that if he was the one, however, you would still be with him, or you would have successfully reunited already. It feels easier to try to work on a relationship with someone who you already know and can get involved with right away. But taking that shortcut doesn't increase your chances of dating success. You need to invest time and energy so you are clear about who and what you really need. Stop wasting time on a dead end.

Mr. Control Freak. He enjoys having a woman around whom he can control and direct. So he will be agreeable toward a fast commitment and relationship. You have to be careful here because you don't want your desire for a relationship to cause you to trade your freedom for one. He knows how to make you feel important and persuade you that your lives depend on each other. Soon you think you can't make it without him (and you don't want to because you wanted a man anyway). Mr. Control Freak often escalates to acting more like Mr. Abuser. And that's a risk you can't afford to take. This man wants you to give up an awful lot to be with him. Resist the urge to jump into a relationship with him.

Mr. Needy. Mr. Needy is lost without a woman. He needs her to do and be so many things for him that he is more likely to want to settle down than other men. Once he settles down, he is going to put his wife to work being his wife, his mother, his accountant, his career coach, and so on. So you need to watch out for him because his willingness to settle down will excite you. He will try to hide just how needy he is so that you will think he really wants to be with you specifically, while really he wants whoever will take him. Don't let his neediness turn you on and lead you to think the two of you will be together forever.

Mr. Under Construction. He is that nice man who looks like he has it all together, but after only a short time you figure out that he doesn't really have any of it together. His whole life is a house of cards, and he is hoping that you get hitched before a strong wind blows his cover and you discover how weak he is inside. As much as you want to settle down, he needs you even more than you need him. You want a man.

You don't want to be a babysitter or constantly have to clean up his messes.

Mr. Abuser. Mr. Abuser needs someone to treat badly. He lives for the opportunity to control and manipulate a woman. As a way to bait a woman into a relationship, he is often very charismatic and sweet when you first start dating. He doesn't show his true hurtful colors until you are already in love or maybe even living together. You have to keep your eyes open for the first signs of him shifting from nice to nasty, and get away as fast as you can. He will promise you the dream commitment you have always wanted, but he won't be able to deliver on it. He is one of the men who wants to settle down even more than you do. If he can find a woman to abuse, then to him a commitment is a small price to pay.

Mr. Addict. Mr. Addict needs you more than you need him. He has addictions that lead to financial and other problems that he needs help resolving. He needs a woman by his side to help him feed his addictions and to pick up the pieces when things fall apart. You want a man, but not this one. He will come on strong, but you have to resist and remember what it is going to cost you for this relationship to work. Hold out for someone who truly gets his highs from being with you.

You are a great person who deserves a great man, but you are unlikely to ever meet him if you are so busy trying to settle down with the first taker. Often the first man willing to settle down is usually the man with the most needs and issues. (The same might be said about you.) A healthy man isn't trying to settle for the first taker or looking to decide after only one or two dates. He wants to take his time and find Ms. Right because he knows he is a catch. You have to start acting like the catch that you are. When you are desperate for a man, you end up settling. Don't sell yourself short!

How You Became Mistyped as Ms. Soul Mate

So how did you become Ms. Soul Mate? You probably started learning how to be her from a very young age. Our society teaches women that their purpose in life is to find a man, get married, have children, and live happily ever after. And some women grow up expecting that exact thing. They work very hard to achieve it and are downright depressed if it hasn't happened yet.

There's nothing wrong with wanting the white picket fence. But if you are unhappy in your life's journey toward that end, then you have a problem. You have to be happy during the ride so that you don't take any shortcuts or accept any male driver to travel along with you. Here are some other experiences you may have had that contributed to you becoming Ms. Soul Mate:

♦ You saw your mother or another woman in your family talking and acting as if she were nothing without her man. If your mother was not with your father, she may have seemed to be on a desperate search for his replacement, looking for someone to be the man around the house.

- If your mom or another family member was a Ms. Soul Mate, you saw that she was always dating someone, and as a result you believed that you should always be dating someone too. If they appeared to have no other goals or life aspirations than to go on another date or to get a man to come over for the night, you may have learned that finding a man was the most important goal for a woman.
- You grew up fantasizing about the day when you would be able to start your own family. Then you could get the love and affection you may have missed as a child, or you could finally be the most important person in someone's life.
- Many of your friends were Ms. Soul Mates. Like many young women, they were the types of girls who lived for dating and seemed to have one boyfriend right after the other.

Even your conversations with male friends or men you dated may have reinforced the belief that women live for relationships, and that it's a bad sign if you aren't in one. Ever heard the question "So, do you have a boyfriend?" and if you say no, the follow-up is, "Why not? What's wrong with you?" This is so silly because there are more single people in the world than not. So is something wrong with all of them? In some people's minds (even if they don't recognize their own feelings because they are so subtle), having no boyfriend equals being a loser.

Everywhere you turn in books and movies, especially in children's fairy tales, knights in shining armor are whisking women away to a beautiful life. Little girls play with toy babies and make-believe kitchen and laundry sets, fully equipped with appliances and play food. How can you not expect some of that to rub off on you? Assuming it has, you don't have to continue to buy into the fantasy or judge yourself harshly for not living it.

I hope you achieve all of your relationship goals, but I don't want you to be miserable waiting for your soul mate to come. Or to be so desperate to find a soul mate that you are convinced that virtually every man you date is him, until you figure out he isn't. Enjoy dating. Don't pressure yourself to settle down so that you commit to Mr. Wrong, or drive yourself into a depression waiting for Mr. Right. If you aren't willing to let go of some of Ms. Soul Mate's bad habits, they are bound to have a negative impact on you and your life.

A Ms. Typed Makeover:
From Ms. Soul Mate to Ms. Date Before You Mate

If you are ready to say goodbye to Ms. Soul Mate, you need to focus on developing a life and identity outside of dating and romantic relationships. Allowing so much of your time and energy to revolve around romance robs you of the opportunity to enjoy all that life has to offer. You are more likely to find the man you're looking for when you stop looking for him and start looking for you. So find yourself first, and all that is lovable about you. If you don't know, how do you expect anyone else to figure it out? When you love yourself and your life as much as you love being in a relationship, you will see a remarkable change in how men treat you. Now is the time to start loving yourself enough to stop running into the arms of any man who will have you. Take your time to fearlessly live while waiting for Mr. Right.

Now that you understand the impact that being Ms. Soul Mate has had on you and your relationships, you can make a break from your old habits so that your future doesn't look like your past. Here are some suggestions for getting started:

Distinguish fact from fantasy. One of the things that gets Ms. Soul Mate in trouble is her enthusiasm for fantasy. She is so caught up in and obsessed with the idea of wanting to find the one perfect man for her that she finds little pleasure in doing much other than that, and more important, she expects her life to unfold like a fairy tale. In most girls' dreams a man shows up to sweep them off their feet, marry them, have beautiful children, and live in a house with a white picket fence. Their wedding will be the most important day of their lives, and it will be perfect and magical.

The truth is that relationships don't develop or look like this. Even if you meet and marry "the one," relationships hit bumps and bruises, and all the planning in the world doesn't protect you from life's problems. You need to get in touch with how real relationships work. Not the movie kind, the celebrity kind, or the soap opera kind—the real kind! Once you realize that finding your soul mate and living the perfect life is not possible, because nothing and no one is perfect, you can stop obsessing and acknowledge that there is more to life than dating.

Be here now. It is so important that you live in the present, not in the future. Sometimes you get so lost in your dreams about your perfect future with your soul mate that you forget to stop and smell the roses along the road to finding him. You can get so caught up in your plan that you lose all the fun, excitement, and happiness you can experience until your plan comes together. As I've said here repeatedly, there is life outside of romantic relationships, and you will have to meet and date many Mr. Wrongs before you meet Mr. Right. Instead of being sad or angry about that, why not embrace it and enjoy all that life has to offer until Mr. Right comes along? If you are out there looking unhappy and cranky because you are single, a good man is going to take one look at your funky expression and move on. You want to exude calm and happiness and let those things attract a happy and healthy man to you.

Dating can be fun if you don't look at it as a punishment for those who don't have a boyfriend. The whole purpose of dating is to date enough different people that you get the opportunity to find the one for you. If you keep trying to settle down with each man you date, how do you expect to be available for "the one"? Enjoy the variety, fun, and attention while you can.

Don't use children as relationship leverage. Sometimes your desire to find your soul mate distorts your decision-making abilities. Some women believe that children are what hold relationships together and that once you have a child with a man it guarantees you a relationship with him. In Ms. Soul Mate's mind, having a child with the man confirms that he must be her soul mate. She thinks that he will want to be with his child, and that means he will have to also be with her. You romanticize what you are doing and think that because you have a child together, the father of your children will be in your life forever. Well, he might be in your life forever, but not necessarily as your boyfriend or husband.

Children don't keep relationships together. The divorce rate and the number of children growing up in single-parent homes proves that having a child together is not enough to keep a man romantically interested in or committed to you. He may always be a father but not always a boyfriend or husband. For that reason, don't even think about rushing into having children (especially if you aren't in a committed long-term relationship) as a way to create a commitment between you and your man. Having children is not going to make your fantasy about being with your soul mate come true, and children don't deserve to be in the middle of this mess. Try to lock in the relationship first, and then add the kids.

Pamper yourself when you're single. You should take care of yourself whether you are in a relationship or not. Too many women pay attention to making important changes and improvements in their lives only when they are trying to impress someone they are interested in romantically. You need to take care of yourself all the time, not just when you care about winning someone over. Make eating right, exercising, relaxing, and being social a regular part of your life, whether a man is with you or not. This sends out the signal that you care for yourself and that you expect the same kind of treatment from the man you date.

Wait before you bare your soul. Many men have been scared away by Ms. Soul Mate's intense focus on marriage and children. Her agenda to settle down can be so strong that before a man can get to know her well enough to consider a second date, she hits him with the M-word. He loses interest right then and there. You might say, "Well, if he isn't interested in those things and I am, shouldn't I find out now? So that we don't waste each other's time?" On the one hand, if you know that you are ready to settle down, you need to know if you are dating a self-proclaimed bachelor for life. But you also need to give a man who is on the fence a chance. Given some time, he may discover a reason to get off it. But if you try to push him off that fence, there's going to be trouble.

For most men, when it comes to relationships, the future can be scary. And in their minds, the future is the next date with you, not becoming your boyfriend or husband. Unlike Ms. Soul Mate, men aren't always walking around planning their weddings. They don't necessarily decide that they are ready to get married until they meet the right woman. For that reason they need time to get to know you. Whether they are ready to get married and have kids depends on how much they like and love the woman they are dating. If they never make it past the first date, then certainly the answer will be no! So rather than show all your cards too soon, wait a date or two and see what you can learn from the rest of his conversation. Men like the chase, so if you offer yourself up too soon, you will likely lose their interest. You want to spoon-feed him information about yourself—it will go down a lot smoother and will bring an air of mystery. Telling him you are ready to get married on a first date is kind of like telling him you haven't had sex in over a year—it's TMI (too much information).

Find your purpose. What defines Ms. Soul Mate is her singular focus on being in a relationship. One of the best ways to break out of that mind-set is to spend some time identifying your life's purpose. There is more to life than men, dating, and relationships. They are a big part of life and a great part of life, but they are not your sole purpose here. You need to get rid of the belief that you have no purpose without a relationship, and that your worth is defined by someone else's romantic desire for you. If you have never stopped to think about your value or purpose, stop and consider what wonderful gifts and talents you have to share with the world. Maybe you are a talented performer, a supportive friend, or a mathematical genius. I know that there is something that you feel passionate about that relates to the beauty and value you add to the world. Figure out what that thing is, and spend more time doing it. It will help you understand what significance to place on dating, when you realize that you offer more to the world than just what you can achieve as someone's girlfriend or wife.

Expand your horizons. In addition to discovering your purpose and passion, you need to expand your horizons. If most of your focus is on dating, you are missing out on a lot that life has to offer. There are countries to visit, friends to make, artwork to paint, promotions at work, degrees to earn, and so on. I want you to imagine all of the different areas of your life including family, friendships, community, religion/spirituality, education, career, and financial health. Then consider all the different goals and aspirations you could pursue in each of those areas. (See the Ms. Typed Makeover Kit for more.) You'll be happier and healthier completing these goals and setting a new course for your life.

Enjoy dating and the single life as much as a committed relationship. Once you get married, you have the rest of your life to *be* married (decades!). So until then, enjoy being single, and have all the fun that can be had dating and discovering different people. Believe me, the grass is always greener in someone else's yard, and once you are in a committed relationship, the time will come when you look at the fun single people are having and wish you were still a part of it. Dating is an opportunity to learn what you like in different men and to work on your issues so that you are prepared for a serious relationship later. When you don't give yourself a chance to date without pursuing a commitment, you rob yourself of that growth opportunity, an opportunity that will prepare you to create a more successful committed relationship when the time is right. Use dating as a time to learn lessons about relationships that you can discover only by making mistakes. Even when dating doesn't result in a relationship, it can lead to new friendships and social connections that can benefit you personally and professionally.

Don't rush to settle down.

Enjoy being single.

Ms. Drama Queen

WHAT SHE LOOKS LIKE

- Thinks that love is supposed to be a challenge and is constantly pursuing difficult relationships that result in rejection.

- Will wait forever for a player, but won't give a good man a chance because he's boring. She thrives on worrying about what he's out there doing wrong.

- Feels motivated by competition with other women. She likes to prove she can take a man from another woman.

- Believes the myth that certain men (the ones who are actually interested in her) aren't her "type," so she won't give them a chance to date her.

◆ Has many other names, including Ms. Asking for Trouble, Ms. Stalker, and Ms. Queen Bee.

Ms. Drama Queen loves a challenge and likes dating only bad boys, unavailable men, or players. She measures how special she is by seeing how hard a man works to get her attention and the extraordinary effort it takes for them to make their relationship work. She pursues unavailable men because of the emotional roller-coaster ride, instead of men who are interested in her and available. Ms. Drama Queen doesn't believe it's love unless you do something dramatic to get it, so that is exactly what she does in an attempt to find the love of her life. She doesn't mind a little unhealthy competition from friends and ex-girlfriends of the man she's dating. If she can't get a rise out of a man, she thinks he doesn't really care.

THE ROLES SHE PLAYS

There are several roles that Ms. Drama Queen plays in relationships, including:

◆ **Ms. I Can Love You Better.** She competes with other women for a man who's not worth having in the first place. He is usually married or already committed to someone else.

◆ **Ms. Negative Attention.** She enjoys jealousy and control because she believes it is a man's way of showing her love and attention.

- **Ms. Asking for Trouble.** She needs the emotional roller-coaster ride to feel the thrill of love. The "nice" guy can't excite her.

- **Ms. Queen Bee.** Her demands are over the top as she selfishly makes herself the center of her dating relationships. A man's job is to cater to her every need and keep her happy, or else she will make his life miserable.

- **Ms. Stalker.** She stops at nothing to chase a man down and sabotage his life outside of their relationship.

> **Just Like You** ....
>
> *Ms. Drama Queen has company in her experience of the relationship roller coaster. Ms. Sex Machine, Ms. Anaconda, and even Ms. Second Place often have, or are motivated by, dramatic relationship experiences too, so you should read their profiles.*

LYNETTE'S STORY

Lynette's best friend Christine tried to hook her up with a nice man she knew from work. He was average looking but nice, responsible, and generous. Lynette had already been in enough troubled relationships, and Christine didn't want to see her get hurt again. Lynette came to visit Christine at work just to get a sneak peek at the man, but after one glance she said no way. She decided that he was too nerdy and not cool or sexy enough for her.

One person who did attract her was Christine's brother Randy. Christine insisted that Lynette stay away from her brother, a self-proclaimed player. He lived in the gym and the nightclub, and Lynette knew it. She had heard a million stories through Christine about the trail of broken hearts Randy left behind. Nevertheless, on a night out without Christine, who did Lynette bump into but Randy. And she could not control the urge to flirt with him. She just knew that if he had the chance to get to know her, she could tame that wild beast! Without Christine there to stop her, one thing led to another, and Lynette and Randy exchanged numbers and hooked up. A string of booty calls later, Lynette was determined to eliminate some of her competition. Before Randy knew it, she had managed to call his daughter's mother on the phone, and then was at the gym giving a few of his personal training clients a piece of her mind as well. When Randy came to her house to confront her about these conversations, they had a heated argument that ended in make-up sex.

Lynette and Randy played a game of cat and mouse for a few more weeks. She would anticipate where he was going, then show up there to sabotage his attempts to talk to other women. Every time he tried to call it off (what little of it there was), she kept reinserting herself into the picture, using sex or gifts to get him back when she had to. The final straw was a barroom confrontation between Lynette and Randy's cousin! By the time she caught up with him that night, she was so drunk that she immediately confronted and almost attacked the woman he was whispering to, who just happened to be his cousin. This time he really did stop seeing her. She kept calling, texting, and making late-night drivebys to see if he had guests, but after four weeks of no response from him, she finally gave up.

So What?

For those of you who live in a more peaceful world, Lynette's story sounds extreme, but among Drama Queens, her story represents only the tip of the iceberg. Why do we care about Lynette dating a sexy hottie like Randy? Don't most women want the hottest man they can get? Yes, most women do want to date a man who they are attracted to and think is sexy and fun. But they also have to be responsible and smart enough to know when they are dating out of their league. Too many women are attracted to these bad boys, but they aren't expecting to be used emotionally or sexually and then tossed aside afterward. As much as she might not want to date a "good" man, Lynette needed to find a middle ground.

In addition to chasing after the wrong type of man (a player who is only going to leave her wanting more), Lynette made things worse by allowing her Ms. Drama Queen to show up and confront strangers, stalk Randy, and rely on sex to glue the relationship together. At some moments she felt a rush of excitement during her busy pursuit of Randy, because she wanted to date someone sexy and desirable. But deep down she was embarrassed by her immature and desperate behavior. All of that excitement ended in humiliation and depression. She even upset Christine when she mistakenly confronted her and Randy's cousin in the club. It was one thing for Randy to be a witness to her madness, but now Christine knew how much drama she could create, and that changed their relationship a bit. Unfortunately for Lynette, as much as she was embarrassed and self-conscious about her behavior, she didn't quite understand why she always crosses that line or know how to stop. So soon after Randy another unsuspecting bad boy came into her life. (His tires were slashed!)

Before Lynette can find the right type of man, she has to get herself together. She needs to know herself better and get to the bottom of why she would rather be in a dramatic relationship than a peaceful one. What does she get out of it? How does it make her feel? She also has to increase the love and affection she feels for herself, so that she is not as dependent on a man to make her feel loved and special. Once she masters these principles, she will pursue less drama in her love life. She can have fewer dramatic dating experiences, set a calmer tone, and lead a relationship down a more peaceful path.

Why It Matters

What are the negative consequences of being mistyped as Ms. Drama Queen?

◆ **You feel embarrassed.** When the drama subsides and you are able to sit back and reflect on how you have behaved and what you have tolerated, you often feel embarrassed: embarrassed by what you did and that you sank so low as to put yourself out there for someone who probably didn't deserve it. When you see on your phone bill that you called twenty-five times in ten minutes, you can't help but feel shame because it makes you look crazy, when you know that you don't want to look that way or act that way.

◆ **You lose self-respect.** When you behave in these overly dramatic ways and go to these lengths, it may make you lose respect for yourself. Upon reflection, you know that you deserve a loving relationship, and you can't understand why you would do things that don't accurately represent who you are or how you want to be perceived. When you are stalking a man and willing to fuss and fight with other women over him, even if it doesn't bother him, it erodes your self-esteem and self-respect. You shouldn't have to disrespect yourself to gain or keep a man, and if that is what keeps you excited and motivated in a relationship, you are definitely a drama queen.

◆ **You cause unnecessary harm to yourself.** Drama queens make decisions that get them into trouble. They don't mind fighting with the man they are dating and with any other woman who dares to cross their path. This could lead to physical confrontations that could cause you to get hurt. Many times these fights are a lot of posturing and yelling, but you never know when it's going to escalate to that next level and you or your personal property are harmed. Many a Drama Queen has had a broken window or been in trouble at work over some senseless phone calls or arguments taking place on the job.

◆ **You get rejected.** Sometimes the drama is started by the man and you tolerate it, and at other times the drama comes from you and he tolerates it. When you bring unnecessary drama, stress, anxiety, and trouble into a man's life, he may not see it as a sign of your deep love for him. And you will end up being hurt and rejected. That is not the tone you want to set or the path you want to walk down. Initially some men (especially Drama Kings) might be turned on and like you. Or he may think that it is exciting to have two women fight for him, or to have a woman practically break her neck to be with him. But even a Drama King and certainly most healthy men are turned off by a controlling, bossy, jealous woman who makes all of his business hers and who isn't happy unless there is some kind of conflict going on between the two of you.

JUST HER TYPE

If you are Ms. Drama Queen, you have a tendency to thrive on challenging dating situations and therefore attract men who bring lots of baggage and dating problems to the table. You are particularly vulnerable to:

Mr. Player. Ms. Drama Queen is vulnerable to players because she already likes a little competition, and with them it's all about fighting for time and attention. She is willing to do whatever it takes to win him over, even if it means dramatic shows of affection for him or nasty fights with the other women in his life. Instead of accepting that he isn't interested in love, relationships, or exclusivity, Ms. Drama Queen enjoys and pursues the challenge of trying to change his mind. Either way, her efforts are usually uncalled for and too extreme and end up embarrassing her and turning the man off (which can send her into another round of dramatic behavior in an attempt to get him to come back to her).

Mr. Unhappily Married. Mr. Unhappily Married is committed to someone else and is practically and emotionally unavailable as a boyfriend, so he throws gasoline on Ms. Drama Queen's fire. She is already emotional and feisty enough—she doesn't need a ready-made fight with this man's wife as payback to him for putting her through all of this. Of course, if she wasn't attracted to drama, she might not be attracted to the battles and challenges that come with dating someone else's husband.

Mr. Pleasure Principle. Good sex can make some women act a little crazy, and Ms. Drama Queen is no exception. After she's with Mr. Pleasure Principle, she has no problem turning into a full-time stalker and searching for him in the daytime with a flashlight. Her natural tendency is to want more, and his unavailability is a setup for disaster.

Mr. Control Freak. Mr. Control Freak pushes all of Ms. Drama Queen's buttons. And they are both very controlling. He is busy trying to control her, while she is doing the same to him. That constant tension makes for the type of drama she likes in her life. They regularly have fights and disagreements over who is right and how things should be done. This combination is a dead end.

Mr. Abuser. Nothing is more dramatic than breaking up and then making up with Mr. Abuser. One minute he is hurtful, and the next he is bending over backward to convince you how much he loves you despite what he put you through. Don't buy it. Mr. Abuser's jealousy and controlling ways come across to Ms. Drama Queen like love. When that's the only kind of "love" you've ever known, it's hard to believe there is something else out there waiting for you.

HOW YOU BECAME MISTYPED AS MS. DRAMA QUEEN

Here are some experiences that may have contributed to you becoming Ms. Drama Queen:

- Some of the young men you dated were quick to argue or get physical, and instead of it turning you off, it turned you on. Or you thought you had no other options so you started to expect it and tolerate it.
- Your friends were drama queens, and you listened to their stories of fighting girls at rival schools over their boyfriends, physical fights with their boyfriends, and cursing arguments. When everyone around you is doing it, dramatic responses to situations appear to be the appropriate way to handle things.
- When it came to disagreements within dating relationships, you observed dramatic fighting followed by romantic make-ups among your parents, parental figures, or other couples in your family, friends, or community.
- In the families of many drama queens there is a lot of

confrontation and yelling, and getting physical may be considered normal, everyday behavior. This was true of your family.

♦ As a child, you observed a lot of conflict in your home or your community and learned to both expect and be comfortable with it.

And let's not forget all of the dramatic portrayals of women setting men's clothes on fire, throwing their things out of windows, pouring drinks over their heads, keying their cars, and slapping them in public. Television and movies depict women acting foolish without showing the real-world consequences to those actions. Somehow, being a drama queen on screen means escaping prosecution and getting back together with the man (who evidently forgives her!). When in real life, drama queens are usually harmed by the man they're dating for acting that way.

None of these examples excuse your behavior, but they may explain when and how you came to the conclusion that it is okay to act this way. Now that you are learning that these actions come at a high price, you can work to make important changes for the better.

A Ms. Typed Makeover:
From Ms. Drama Queen to
Ms. Calm, Cool, and Collected

Now is the time to focus on seeking balance and peace in your life. When you become accustomed to a less stressful life, you will be less attracted to and tolerant of drama in your dating relationships. You will have to stop thinking and believing that life is more interesting, exciting, and fun when it is filled with problems and overemotionality. Some women grew up under very stressful circumstances, so to them high-conflict relationships are the norm. Redefine that norm, and pursue healthy relationships with less fear, anxiety, and disappointment.

Drama has become a regular part of all aspects of your life. While you are dating, you have to remember who and what triggers this button. Sometimes you know intellectually what you need to do differently, but you will still need to put a lot of effort into breaking your old habits. Here is what can help:

Find ways to relieve stress. Instead of being charged up by stress, you need to learn to enjoy being relaxed. Relaxation needs to become the new normal for you. When you get stressed or someone upsets you, try working out, meditating or praying, practicing yoga, or taking a hot bubble bath. If you're at work and you have only a couple minutes to yourself, then take a walk to the ladies' room or get a cup of tea or a decaf coffee as a way to walk off the stress and calm down. You'll be able to regain your composure and get back to work.

Stop right there. When someone does something to upset you, before you have time to think, your body already seems to be moving toward that person to give them a piece of your mind. You have to resist the urge to lash out or to let your emotions get out of whack. As soon as you feel the instinct to march off and do something over the top, stop. Take some deep breaths. Don't call anyone, don't confront anyone. Instead take a walk and take some time to calm down. Give yourself time to think through a nondramatic response to your situation.

Try dating a nice, safe, peaceful man. Give a nice man a chance. That sounds boring already, right? Then you better redefine what bores you and what excites you! You enjoy the roller-coaster ride so much that when someone who could meet many of your relationship needs comes along, you aren't interested if he is wrapped up in a nice man package. Being an emotionally charged man doesn't make him a better partner, but that emotional energy attracts you. You see it as passion instead of drama. Well, forget about that. I know you won't make the change overnight, but for every drama king you date, give a nice man a chance too.

Learn when to back down, give up, and let go. Part of being Ms. Drama Queen means you don't know when to give up the fight. You want what you want, and you refuse to stop when you don't get it, or accept no for an answer. Sometimes in life you are just not going to get what you want—that is life. Instead of continuing to fight to the death, you need to learn to compromise and accept when a situation is not going your way. The drama queen in you has adult temper tantrums when things don't work out. Instead of doing that, why don't you try looking clearly at the situation? How important is it really? Does it truly make any long-lasting difference if you don't get your way? Soon you'll learn to recognize when you aren't going to get your way and just let it go.

Apologize after a dramatic outburst. When you have overstepped your boundaries and done something hurtful to someone you love or something that embarrasses you, you know. Rather than sweep it under the rug and pretend it never happened, start by acknowledging to yourself that you were wrong. When you come to terms with it, approach whomever you offended and apologize. At a minimum say that you are sorry for how you acted (or overreacted), and if you want, you can also explain why you did it, despite your current understanding of how irrational it was. An apology lets the person know that you didn't intend to behave so terribly and reassures them that you will try hard not to act that way in the future.

Get over the bad boys. Our culture glorifies and promotes bad boys, but they bring out the worst in you. The bossy, controlling, abusive player and commitment-phobic types create a dramatic roller-coaster ride in a relationship, and trying to get along with them pushes all of your buttons. Fighting to be important in their lives and wrestling with them for freedom and control gets your blood boiling—and is a recipe for verbal and physical disaster. The best way to avoid having your dramatic buttons pushed is to avoid these men and to redefine what you are hoping to experience. The more you learn to relax and enjoy not fighting, the more fussing and fighting will feel uncomfortable to you. It takes time to get used to the quiet, but you'll get there, and you'll get to love and enjoy it.

Redefine what love is and what it looks like. Part of what allows you to be Ms. Drama Queen is the belief that dramatic behavior is a reflection of love. Don't misinterpret a man's jealousy, possessiveness, and controlling nature as love, concern, or affection. The more you think that conflict is love, the more you will look for it, and the more you will try to create it. Make sure that you don't do things to encourage him to be overdramatic or lead him to think that his dramatic behavior is how you measure his love.

Refuse to fight over any man. You need to create a rule that says you aren't going to fight over a man (or with him) about anything. When a man is flirting or cheating with another woman, the man's girlfriend often will immediately get mad at the woman. Sometimes she may want to confront her or even physically fight her! What's really crazy about it is that the girlfriend is angry at the wrong person. Her boyfriend owes her the commitment; he's in the relationship—and is responsible for his actions. If you ever get an urge to call or text a woman whose number is in your boyfriend's phone or to confront her in person, be clear. Your boyfriend is the problem, not the woman. Don't dishonor and disrespect yourself by fighting another woman for him. If he doesn't want to be in a committed relationship with you, then start looking for someone else. Anything else will just make you feel worse about yourself.

Mind your mouth. Ms. Drama Queen is known for a good verbal throwdown. You probably know how to read your man thoroughly and can insult him and his mama before he even realizes what you said. Those insults and verbal combat just escalate disagreements and make your relationship worse. Set a different tone. Lower your voice, end the insults, and communicate in a calm and reasonable manner. If you are yelling because he is yelling over you, then wait until he stops yelling to speak. The two of you obviously aren't listening to each other anyway. Mean things you say can't be taken back. And even though a man may not make a big deal out of it right away, he may remember and hold a grudge. If you talk to him this way because it is how he talks to you, then you should be looking for a new boyfriend. And if you are verbally abusing him, don't think he isn't keeping his eyes open and looking for a new girlfriend. Most men won't put up with it for long.

Find alternative ways to vent your frustration. Your typical way of dealing with frustration might be to argue, yell, call names, insult, push, grab, scratch, or slap. You may invade your man's privacy, damage his things, or withhold your affection. Instead of doing things that will hurt him in the short term but will hurt you and your relationship in the long term, you need to look for healthier alternatives for communicating. If you have a hard time talking about your feelings or getting your point across, try to wait until you calm down to express yourself; wait for a peaceful time to talk once you're both calm; say how you feel without yelling or making insults; and lastly, if you can't successfully talk without arguing, write him a letter expressing your feelings, then edit it to make sure it is not insulting or rude before you share it.

Refuse to share a man. One of the dating situations that encourages you to act like Ms. Drama Queen is sharing a man. If you and your man are not in a monogamous relationship, or if you are supposed to be in a monogamous relationship and he regularly cheats on you, you need to get out. You are never going to be okay with sharing your man, and why should you be? You need to make it clear that this doesn't work for you and if things don't change in the relationship, you have to move on. Why? Because the anger you feel while having to share a man with another woman will drive you to act crazy! Cheating turns the sane you into Ms. Drama Queen, out there stalking your boyfriend, frantically checking his phone and e-mails, or confronting women you see him talking to. When you feel hurt and betrayed, you want to take someone down, and that is a risk you can't afford to take.

Don't allow drama to enter the workplace. Not only do you have to maintain your composure when having disagreements with your manager or coworkers, but you need to make a rule of not allowing any of your personal drama to enter your work life. That means not allowing the men you are dating to visit you at work or even call you there if the two of you are arguing, as it could cause a disturbance. The people at your job don't need to know your relationship problems, and they definitely shouldn't be observing. If you must take a call or meet where you know a dramatic conversation will happen, then leave and take a walk far away, where you can speak freely to that person without your coworkers hearing or witnessing it. Unless you have some tried-and-true long-term friendships with your coworkers, you should also avoid discussing your personal life with them. Hearing about some of the drama that goes on in your personal life might taint people's perception of your professional abilities. Try to keep your work face on at work and keep gossip about you to a minimum.

Seek professional help. You may find that no matter how hard you try, you keep acting out. You don't mean to, you apologize afterward, and yet you still act out over and over. You realize that it is having a negative impact on your life and relationships. If this is the case, then you should consider seeking professional help. You may have anger, anxiety, or depression that is fueling your dramatic responses to situations, and it is hard for some people to get those emotions under control. On the other hand, if you don't see a problem with your out-of-control verbal outbursts or physical attacks, you still need to seek some help. If one relationship after another is going down the drain, even if you think your behavior is justified, why not check in with a mental health professional for an objective perspective and some help with solving your problems for good?

Ms. Bag Lady

What She Looks Like

♦ Has a strong emotional and unrealistic response to normal dating experiences.

♦ Allows her past relationships to breed negative expectations for her current and future relationships.

♦ Hasn't resolved her personal mental health issues, which causes her to be very insecure and overly emotional in relationships.

♦ Gets so stuck in her ways that she doesn't realize that despite her painful past relationships, she hasn't raised her standards or changed her behavior since then. So history is bound to repeat itself.

- Gets criticized, mistreated, and sometimes abused by the men she dates. She tolerates unacceptable behavior like infidelity because she feels that she has no other options, nor the ability to influence the situation.

- Doesn't reveal her weaknesses or show her true self because she fears being taken advantage of, rejected, embarrassed, or mistreated.

- Allows men to take advantage of her because she doesn't want to be single.

- Is controlled by the men in her life but doesn't feel confident or capable enough to take charge of the situation or her life. She doesn't take responsibility for her role and behavior in a relationship.

- Has many other names including Ms. All Cried Out and Ms. Emotional Roller Coaster.

Ms. Bag Lady has a load of emotional baggage and lets her old emotions get played out in her current relationships. She focuses on the relationship as a way to ignore negative feelings, including low self-esteem, anxiety, anger, and resentment. By doing this she allows the unresolved problems of the past to ruin her present and future. When the relationship is abusive, she becomes passive and tolerates the pain. When the relationship isn't abusive, she may be more aggressive and overreact to situations. Even when things in the relationship are going well, she is too emotional, instead of having a more reasonable and less extreme reaction to normal situations. It's as if the nice man gets punished for what the last man did wrong. Sometimes she experiences episodes of unexplained crying, anger, and sadness in response to typical dating experiences like lateness, canceled dates, or unreturned phone calls. Deep down she often feels like no one really loves her or is there for her, and she expects everyone will hurt or eventually disappoint her.

Ms. Bag Lady's emotional state and past experiences make her vulnerable to mistreatment and abuse. As much as she wants to get away from men who treat her badly, mistreatment has become a part of her reality, and much to her confusion, she is attracted to controlling and abusive men. Because so many of the men she dates turn out to be abusive, she finds it very hard to trust men, so when she does finally meet someone who isn't abusive, she doesn't know how to behave. All her negative memories and expectations get in the way of finally dating someone who isn't out to harm her.

THE ROLES SHE PLAYS

There are several roles that Ms. Bag Lady plays in relationships, including:

♦ **Ms. Vulnerable.** Because of her past experiences and emotional injuries, she is vulnerable to being harmed physically and emotionally in relationships.

♦ **Ms. All Cried Out.** She overreacts to lateness, disagreements, unreturned phone calls, and other uncomfortable but not atypical relationship experiences, with tears and threats.

◆ **Ms. Hard Nut to Crack.** She is distrustful and anxious based on past relationship disappointments. She creates arbitrary rules about what she will and won't do based on her bad past relationships.

◆ **Ms. Emotional Roller Coaster.** She lives in constant fear and anticipation of the relationship ending. This causes her to panic and overreact to any sign of change.

◆ **Ms. I've Fallen and I Can't Get Up.** Believes she is in love and feels incapable of controlling her feelings or her relationship. She denies her power and becomes emotionally out of control.

Just Like You ....

The heavy load of old emotions Ms. Bag Lady is carrying around with her causes her to demonstrate many of the characteristics of the other dating types at different times. She is often struggling to make her dating relationships work despite her emotional baggage, which results in her using all kinds of strategies to get and keep a man. Carrying around that baggage could lead her to become Ms. Sex Machine or Ms. Second Place. If you are Ms. Bag Lady, you should read about all other dating types so that you can become aware of the challenges that they are facing, and you can make sure that your emotional state doesn't make you vulnerable to their negative experiences as well.

Tracy's Story

Tracy was at home in bed, hysterically crying. Two days before, she and her boyfriend Todd had a fight, and he threw her against the wall. He told her he was sick and tired of her, left her apartment, and hadn't called her since then. She had no idea what she should do next. Since the fight she had been calling him nonstop apologizing for her behavior, telling him she loved him, and begging him to call her back or come over. She even promised to be a better girlfriend, despite the fact that he hit her in the middle of a fight over him dating his ex-girlfriend again. She laid in her bed and cried and wished that she had a clue what was wrong with her. Why was this happening? When she started thinking about Todd and her last few boyfriends, she was overwhelmed with embarrassment and fear.

She couldn't believe the trend in her behavior—everyone she was dating was aggressive and controlling. She was embarrassed to admit that she had allowed herself to be mistreated for so long. She was afraid that she couldn't stop. Some of the men were psychologically abusive; others were physically abusive. In each relationship she saw signs early on that each man was too possessive, and she explained it away as "love." Once she told her best friend Rebecca about her ex Carl, "Oh girl, you know he loves me—that's why he calls me all the time. He's not checking up on me. He just wants to make sure I made it here safely." And then they had another conversation about her ex Jeff. "It's really all my fault. He grabbed me because I don't know when to shut up." And another time she complained about her ex Derek. "I pushed him into her bed—I should have done what he told me to do." It was shocking for her to recall all the lies she told herself to make her relationships seem okay and to give her an excuse to continue them. She was finally realizing how her experiences of abuse as a child and feelings of low self-esteem led her to be attracted to men who were possessive, abusive, and manipulative. It was easy for Rebecca to tell Tracy to change, but it was really hard for her to make change happen.

So What?

Tracy needed help and fast. She was in a lot of pain, and even though at first she hadn't realized the extent of her problem, she was finally waking up to the reality that she didn't have to tolerate this kind of abuse. Having been abused as a child, Tracy was familiar with the emotional, spiritual, and psychological manipulation that is part of the process. She never received any professional help, though, with processing her feelings and healing. So she still walked around feeling wounded and defective. She blamed herself for her experiences as a child, and she continued to blame herself for her abusive experiences as an adult. This made her even more vulnerable to men who are looking for someone to hurt and manipulate. Even when the relationship she was in was not abusive, she brought all her past feelings of negativity, distrust, and shame into it. Carrying around a lot of negative emotions wreaked havoc on her love life and often under-mined even her healthier relationships.

As much as Tracy wanted to set the tone in relationships and lead the men she dated down the path toward treating her right, she really struggled with self-esteem and loving her-self, the absence of which made it very difficult for her to stand up for herself. She couldn't yet achieve the healthy foundation necessary to have a healthy relationship. Before she could draw more positive men and experiences into her life, she had to start understanding herself better, so that she could heal her wounds and rebuild her life in a way that would invite and allow more positive people and opportuni-ties to come into her world.

Why It Matters

If you have been mistyped as Ms. Bag Lady, what are the nega-tive consequences of holding on to your emotional baggage?

◆ **You experience emotional instability.** Until you find a way to work through all the emotions you have carried around for so many years, you may find yourself riding an emotional roller coaster all the time. It becomes hard to know whether you are having an emotional reaction to something you just experienced, or if your experience is just reminding you of something in the past that is what you are really reacting to.

◆ **You have negative expectations.** When you haven't re-solved your feelings about your past disappointments, you often expect new people you meet to let you down as well. As a result you go around expecting the worst from people and relationships. That expectation brings more disappointing experiences and manifests itself in your overreacting to situations and being guarded or overly negative in your interactions with men. Your negative expectations can also lower the bar for the men you date. Because you asked for so little, you end up not having your relationship needs met.

◆ **You overreact and burn out emotionally.** When you are already feeling angry or depressed, something small can easily upset you and cause you to overreact. This can cause you problems anywhere in life and can definitely work to undermine your dating relationships, when a man can't understand why something so small or so simple would send you over the edge.

◆ **You feel unworthy.** The longer you date men who treat you poorly, the more likely you are to believe that you are unworthy. Once you start to believe that, even long after such a man is gone, those feelings stay with you, and you carry them into each new relationship you enter. Instead of starting new relationships with confidence and excitement, you start them with anxiety and insecurity. Even though the new man doesn't know why you are acting that way, he notices it. So now not only are your feelings of unworthiness affecting you, but they are influencing your new relationship as well. Don't worry, in time you will heal and be healthy enough to attract new men and experiences into your life.

◆ **You make yourself vulnerable to mistreatment.** When you are in an emotionally compromised state of being, you don't feel well or think clearly, so you are more likely to make poor dating decisions. If you are still hurt, angry, resentful, and distrustful as a result of abuse in a past relationship, you will be vulnerable to attracting another abusive man until you resolve those feelings and get to a healthier place. Abusers know how to manipulate. If one sees that you are already feeling low, he can figure out how to convince you to give him a chance. When you have processed and resolved old feelings, however, not only are you happier and healthier, but when men who are nothing but bad news approach you, you can see right through their attempts to manipulate you and turn them down flat.

JUST HER TYPE

If you are Ms. Bag Lady, given your dissatisfaction with yourself and your life, you often attract the types of men who present the challenge of being hard to get, are abusive, or manipulate your negative emotions. You need to be mindful of your vulnerability to:

Mr. Abuser. You are vulnerable to Mr. Abuser because he knows how to manipulate you into trusting him, only to ultimately disappoint you by being dishonest and hurtful. Despite how unhealthy he is, you are used to dealing with his type, and on some levels you are more comfortable with him because you already know what to expect. A relationship with him will include criticism, threats, physical, sexual, or emotional abuse, and more.

Mr. Player. Because Mr. Player dates so many different women, he taps into your fear of being betrayed and mistreated. When he dates other women, you know that it is going to hurt you, but you respond to the challenge anyway, hoping that you can be strong enough to deal with it, rather than decide that he simply isn't the right type of man for you. His lack of interest in relationships leaves you feeling unloved and unlovable. The more you have to fight for his attention and commitment, the worse you feel about yourself, and the more emotional you become. He feeds that little voice in your head telling you that you will never meet the man of your dreams and that you are doomed to be alone. You have to shut that voice up, so you also have to leave him alone.

Mr. Money. He has the wealth and the power, so with you he is in the control seat. You are vulnerable to him because he is so much more confident and accomplished. His strength makes you feel weak. You believe that you aren't good enough for him. Dealing with him makes you feel insecure, and you fear that he will trade you for someone younger and more attractive. When the two of you are together, he is trying to have fun in the moment, while you are stuck worrying about when something bad is going to happen to your relationship.

Mr. Addict. Mr. Addict has the potential to be very hurtful to you emotionally and physically as he struggles with his addictions. He often loses control under the influence, takes advantage of you, and is unreliable. These things magnify your fears that men can't be trusted and they will eventually betray you. When you are dating him, you will be riding that emotional roller coaster, never knowing what negative thing is about to happen next. Since his addictions come first in his life, being with him makes you feel even more unworthy.

THE DOCTOR IS IN

Rachel asked for advice at my online advice column, Ask Dr. Michelle (www.drmichelle.com). She is dealing with what many women, including Ms. Bag Lady, face when trying to get back into the dating game:

DEAR DR. MICHELLE,

My last boyfriend treated me really bad. He used to call me names and hit me sometimes. Since we broke up, I haven't dated anyone in over a year. I want to start dating again, but I'm afraid of meeting the wrong type of guy and getting hurt. What can I do to make sure that I start things out right this time?

DEAR RACHEL,

You are not alone in feeling like you don't know where to start when it comes to the dating game. It's important to sit back and think about how to approach love in a healthy way. Here are some things you should keep in mind when reentering the world of dating:

1. Give yourself some time to heal and recover from the pain of your old relationship. It is very important to start a relationship from a healthy place, so you have to work on healing yourself and processing the

emotions from your last relationship, before you can successfully share love with someone new.

2. Think about what worked or didn't work in your last relationship and what you would like to do differently in a new relationship. Keep these things in mind when you decide who you should date and what you won't allow to happen again. Sometimes you get into a new relationship and re-create the same problems you had in your last relationship. Keep fresh in your mind the types of situations and problems that you want to avoid or that you won't tolerate. Look for warning signs that indicate you are heading down that old road again. When you see things going that way, put your foot down, and if necessary, walk away.

3. Change your life in ways that will allow you to be a better partner. You attract what you are about, so if you don't make certain changes in your life (finances, job, education, spirituality, family, mental health, etc.) you are going to attract the same type of relationship problems and the same type of partner that you might need to avoid. If you meet someone with the same kind of problems or drama that your ex had, don't feel obligated to date that person, even if he is interested in you. Get your life together so that you don't feel needy or dependent on someone in a way that will cause you to use poor judgment out of desperation or put you in harm's way.

How You Became Mistyped as Ms. Bag Lady

If you are Ms. Bag Lady, you have had years of passive learning and experiences that have influenced and taught you to become the way you are today. Starting all the way back to when you were a young child, you may have experienced or observed things that led you down this path, including:

- As a child you were neglected, mistreated, or abused (psychologically, physically, or sexually) by someone in your family or a family friend. When you learn as a young person that the people closest to you cannot be trusted, because they hurt you or fail to protect you, you approach your other relationships with fear and anxiety.
- You observed your mother act like Ms. Bag Lady in her dating relationships.
- Your father or the father figure in your life was mean, controlling, or abusive, and you grew up feeling afraid of men and expecting your future boyfriends and husband to treat you the way your father treated you or your mother.
- Your friends were in very emotional relationships with a lot of yelling or physical fighting, and you thought that was normal and expected the same things to happen to you.
- As you started dating, the first boys you dated were abusive or controlling, so you thought that all boys

were that way, or that something was wrong with you that made boys abuse you or treat you poorly.

◆ Emotional and psychological problems were ignored in your family, so you never learned that they are solvable problems and that it is okay to seek help.

◆ The men you've dated have been abusive or neglectful.

As much as people speak out against abuse and mistreatment, it is still very common in our society, and there are still many people who believe it is justified or who simply won't get involved to help a person they see in trouble. Many women find themselves in danger of physical or psychological harm, yet there still isn't enough talk about how you can get yourself out of such a difficult situation. Women are taught to stick by their man and be very tolerant of whatever they encounter at his hands. Many different influences can lead women into hurtful situations. And even if they don't experience more hurt, they can struggle to cope with the pain that they have already lived through.

Be assured, you can overcome your past hurts and live a happy and healthy life with love in it!

Dating Violence Resources ....

*There are several things you should do if you are in a psychologically or physically violent or abusive relationship. Despite what the man you're dating tells you, be clear about the fact that the abuse is **not** your fault, and that changing your own behavior will **not** stop his abusive behavior. He can make you feel guilty and* responsible for his behavior when you are not responsible for what he does, and nothing you do makes you deserve being abused. He may tell you that you did something to make him do it and that if you changed he wouldn't do it again, but he would just find another excuse and continue his behavior. The most important thing for you to do is educate and protect yourself.

If you think you might be in an abusive relationship, you can start by learning what an abusive relationship looks like and how to recognize the warning signs. Many people think that a relationship is abusive only if it involves punching or hitting. But there are many different forms of psychological, physical, and sexual abuse that can cause you physical and emotional harm, even if you think it's no big deal.

You should also let your partner know that you will not tolerate his behavior. If he doesn't stop, you need to create a safety plan for how to safely get out of the relationship. You should identify a friend or a family member who can support you emotionally and practically as you make a plan to safely end the relationship. A safety plan includes you planning how to escape a violent situation safely, identifying ways to stay safe in your home, finding safe ways to get to and from work or school, and having a safe place to go when abuse happens.

You have a right to be in a safe and healthy relationship. If that is not how you would describe your current dating situation, it's time for you to take action. Here are some resources you can use to help you:

The National Domestic Violence Hotline
  1-800-799-SAFE (7233) (24 hours),
  www.ndvh.org

Rape Abuse & Incest National Network
  1-800-656-HOPE (4673) (24 hours),
  www.rainn.org

The Safe Space
  www.thesafespace.org

A MS. TYPED MAKEOVER: HOW TO GO FROM MS. BAG LADY TO MS. BAGGAGE-FREE

If you are tired of being mistyped as Ms. Bag Lady, you will have to stay focused on processing all the negative thoughts and emotions from your past relationships, romantic or otherwise. It's not that you will forget your past; instead, you will make peace with it. You need to reach the point where you stop ruminating about the past, and when you do think about it, those thoughts don't affect your present-day happiness. Now that you more fully understand how your past may be affecting your present, here are some suggestions that can help you move toward getting more of what you truly want and need today:

Find the source of the pain. One of the most frustrating parts of being Ms. Bag Lady is when you are unclear about how it all started. Over time your emotional pain starts to have a snowball effect, so that even when you name an experience, you may not be thinking about how it, combined with several others, explains why you are so hurt. You need to think about how your experiences with your parents, childhood friends, boyfriends, family, coworkers, and the people in your community have shaped and influenced you. You need to understand yourself better. Once you figure out what hurt you and why it hurt so much, you can start to work on healing. It feels scary at first to allow yourself to travel back in time and relive painful memories, but it's worth it when you realize how much your life will change when you can process your feelings.

Get professional help. It is so important that you rid yourself of the anger and sadness of the past, so that your head and heart are free to love and be loved. Part of the reason you have not been able to avoid some of your abusive experiences or even get your emotions under control may be because you need professional help. It is always assumed that we can just shake off our bad feelings and make them go away, but that is not often the case. If you have been suffering from something like anxiety or depression for a prolonged period of time, those emotions have probably had a huge influence on the way you behaved in your relationships. Even if there were times in the past when you could handle things on your own, you still may sometimes need the assistance of a mental health professional. You aren't a psychologist, so why do you expect to be able to do the job of one? Let someone help you heal in ways that will not only get rid of the negative feelings from the past but also help you make healthier decisions for your future.

Wait before you date. One way you are vulnerable to being hurt is by getting too close and intimate too soon. You need to be friends with some of these men first. Just hang out without the romance. Find out how he treated his last girlfriend or how he responds to stress or disagreements. Don't allow yourself to fall in love so quickly that you never take the time to make sure the man is worthy of your trust and love. I know that is hard because you may feel that you need male companionship now, but you need to resist the urge to move too fast. If you wait, the warning signs will show themselves. And you will be able to safely eliminate someone from your life, before they have the opportunity to really hurt you physically or emotionally. Set the tone in your relationship and determine how quickly you want things to move ahead. Slow down and lead the man you're dating onto a friendship path until you are sure that you should pursue romance.

Don't confuse the past with the present. When you haven't resolved your negative feelings about your past, you usually go into your next relationship feeling insecure and distrustful. Suppose you find a nice man to date who acts loving and hasn't given you any reason to doubt him—you are likely to push him away if you always act defensively and treat him as if he can't be trusted. Sometimes you may not even realize that you are doing it. You may be giving your new boyfriend a hard time because your old boyfriend gave you a hard time. Before you jump to conclusions and make things hard on your new man, ask yourself if your feelings and behaviors are based on how he is acting or on your fear of him starting to act like someone you once knew. Instead of becoming defensive and distrustful, try staying calm and acting as if you expect him to do the right thing by you. If you expect men to do wrong, they know you expect it, and it may make them feel it's okay to misbehave. When you act as if you believe that he knows he better not try any funny business, then you set a tone that says you expect him to act right, and if he doesn't, he will have to answer to you!

Balance your expectations. Your difficult life experiences sometimes throw your dating expectations out of balance. On the one hand, you sometimes expect way too much from a man, are overly sensitive, and overreact to things. On the other hand, you expect way too little from a man or tolerate his psychological and physical abuse or neglect and other inappropriate behavior. You need to find the balance between the two. You don't want to make a mountain out of a molehill, but you also don't want to ignore the elephant in the room, especially when your health is at risk. When you are in a calm place and can think very logically and rationally, sit down and list men's behaviors that you consider either desirable or unacceptable. That way when you are in the heat of the moment and are allowing your boundaries to be very loose, you can refer back to your list and remind yourself of what you said you should do when certain things happened. That way you will know, for example, whether to be so upset about an unreturned phone call or whether to be so calm about being verbally assaulted.

Wait before you respond. Ms. Bag Lady has a tendency to overreact to relatively normal situations. Before you get too upset with the man you are dating, take a breath and give yourself a few minutes to calm down and think rationally about your situation. If you can hold back the tears or the yelling and think, you may realize that you are overreacting and that your thoughts and assumptions are overly negative and unlikely. If he doesn't return your phone call right away, you need to consider the realistic reasons why he may be unavailable and not assume that he is doing it because he doesn't want to talk to you, is with another woman, or doesn't care about your feelings. If you are patient enough, you will eventually talk and find out the truth. So don't send yourself on an unnecessary emotional roller coaster of worry in the meantime.

Spend more time with those who are good to you. Many people, both male and female, may have hurt and disappointed you. However, if you look around your life, there are probably some who have always been nice to you, whom you may not have given a chance to play a larger role in your life. Now is the time for you to give these folks some more of your attention and allow them to be supportive and loving. Maybe it's a man who you thought was too boring and nice to date, or maybe it's a quiet friend at work who you've never hung out with but seems like she might be cool. Sometimes we choose our friends and lovers based on the wrong criteria. If you have grown accustomed to being rejected and neglected, you may attract men and women who are selfish and controlling, but you pursue relationships with them anyway. Instead, choose some of the people who may not be as challenging but are a whole lot more loving. If there isn't anyone like that already in your life, keep your eyes open for them. When you meet someone new, ask yourself: Based on what I know about this person, is he or she a good candidate to become a supportive lover or a loving friend?

Stop blaming yourself. Ms. Bag Lady often blames herself for the bad things she has experienced in life. This makes her feel worse about herself and even more emotional. None of those bad things were your fault. Even if you feel like you tolerated a bad situation for too long, there is no reason to keep blaming yourself for what happened. Chances are that you did the best you could with what you knew at the time. Now that you know more, you can do more. Don't you dare waste your time and energy feeling ashamed of what you have been through! You are a survivor, and you should be proud to have survived. You may not feel that you handled things the way you wanted to, and that's fine. Now is your opportunity to evolve and make your old ways a thing of the past.

Ms. Mom

What She Looks Like

◆ Focuses on solving a man's problems while ignoring her own. Paying a little more attention to solving her own problems would help her attract a more responsible and mature man.

◆ Takes on a man's problems and goals because they seem easier to accomplish than her own.

◆ Acts as an enabler, giving a man what he wants instead of encouraging him to get it for himself.

◆ Thinks that if she takes care of the man she's dating now, he will eventually take care of her later. But he won't. Instead he will keep expecting her to do everything.

◆ Is supportive, loyal, and committed. Her challenge is to not give away too much to the man she's dating because she fears that he stays with her only for what she does instead of for who she is.

◆ Also known as Ms. Life Coach.

M s. Mom tries to mother her man and solve his problems, when she needs to focus that self-improvement energy on herself. She usually attracts men whose lives are a work in progress. When the man she is dating needs help getting his life on track, she is more than willing to help him every step of the way. For every step he takes toward fulfilling his responsibilities and goals, she gladly takes ten more. She also thinks she can "buy" love with all of her support and attention. She believes her generosity is a guarantee that she will keep her man. She is disappointed when she discovers that despite her extraordinary efforts and commitment, she often ends up alone, feeling physically and emotionally depleted, with unpaid loans and a broken heart.

There are several Ms. Mom roles that women play in relationships, including:

Ms. Saint. She spends so much time on the man she's dating that she neglects herself. His improvement becomes her priority, and she's willing to make whatever sacrifices are necessary, even sacrificing her own needs, to help him meet his goals.

Ms. Psychotherapist. She believes she can resolve a man's deep emotional issues. She thinks she can counsel and love away the problems of his past, whether it is a broken heart from his first love or anger from abuse during childhood. She believes it is her responsibility to heal him and put him back together. But his problems are neither her responsibility nor within her control to change.

Ms. Life Coach. He promises to work on something, and she does all the work. She is his personal assistant, lawyer, accountant—you name it. If he needs a new job, she can find it, write his résumé, coach him on what to say during the interview, be a personal reference, and call in sick for him. When does she have time for her own career? She doesn't—either that or she doesn't sleep.

Ms. Makeover. She thinks she can change a man into her own personal dream. She tries to change his looks, his career, and if she's really on a roll, his overall personality. She will take on changing him from couch potato to metrosexual, from grunge to prep, from blue collar to white collar, or from wallflower to life of the party.

Just Like You ....

> *Who else is like Ms. Mom? Ms. Mom often has the same dating challenges as Ms. Second Place. Both types have a strong desire to please. If you are Ms. Mom, be sure to check out Ms. Second Place. Ms. Rose-Colored Glasses has an unwillingness to see and*

accept what is truly going on within a relationship. Once she finally realizes what her man is lacking, she sometimes starts acting like Ms. Mom, as a way to compensate for his shortcomings, so read about Ms. Rose-Colored Glasses, too.

JENN'S STORY

Jenn was having the time of her life dating a coworker named David. He was a sexy, young, life-of-the-party type man whom everyone liked. They got to know each other one night after work when a bunch of people from the office went out for drinks. At the end of the night she asked who needed a ride home, and David took her up on her offer. They had a great conversation on the way home. Jenn discovered that they lived near each other and that he didn't have a car. He said he had been saving to buy one and would probably have it by the end of the month. So she offered to give him a ride to work until he got his new car. Soon afterward they started dating. It wasn't long before he started asking to borrow her car on a regular basis. When she knew he wanted it, she bought gas and took it to the car wash. It never came back clean or with the gas tank refilled. She didn't mind because it seemed temporary, and after all, he was her boyfriend, so she was happy to do it for him.

When David started complaining about his small apartment and annoying roommate, Jenn suggested he move in with her. He said he really didn't want to, that he wanted his own place and had already called about renting an apartment. But she insisted that he come stay with her at least until he signed the lease on his new place.

After several months it seemed as if the plans for David's new car and apartment were long forgotten. Jenn had never discussed with David any rules for using her car, or even anything about him paying his share of the rent. Partly, it was because she didn't expect the situation to be permanent and also because she had been happy to be in a relationship and so enjoyed sharing her things, at least at first. But after months passed, she began to feel angry and believed that David was taking advantage of her. He came and went in her car as he pleased. He acted as if the responsibility of paying the rent didn't even exist. And while all of this was happening, she was doing all the household chores and paying all the household bills. In the back of her mind she knew that this relationship was costing her some of the money she was supposed to be saving to go back to school, but she feared that if she stopped doing all the work in the relationship, David would break up with her.

Jenn couldn't figure out why she hadn't picked up on the fact that David was a moocher when she met him. Part of her resented that he wasn't doing more to help out financially, and another part of her kind of enjoyed taking care of him. Most of the time David didn't acknowledge Jenn's hard work. But every time she got really fed up with doing things for him, he would tell her how much he loved and needed her. Those words were all she needed to keep her going. Hearing his appreciation for what she did for him made her feel special, important, and loved, and that kept her going for a while.

As much as she didn't want to rock the boat with David, she eventually reached a point where she could no longer pick up his slack. She had already spent most of the money she saved for tuition and started to resent how one-sided her relationship with David had become. When she finally spoke up for herself and asked him to pitch in, he became very defensive and threatened to move out. She broke down and told him she was sorry, and to forget about what she said, but he still left. Jenn was devastated.

So What?

So why do we care if Jenn wanted to be David's sugar mama, especially since he was her boyfriend? We care because while she was so busy trying to mother him and solve his problems, she didn't realize that the habits and patterns that she was creating between them were ultimately not going to be relationship-promoting. Taking care of David might have been fun at first, but after a while she resented the lack of balance in their interactions. That imbalance undermined their relationship. It never occurred to Jenn that her insistence on solving all of David's problems for him led her to this difficult place. She opened the door to him taking advantage of her by not being willing to discuss her own wants, needs, and expectations regarding her things and her home. She made it far too easy for him to change his plans of independence, to stop taking care of himself, and just to allow her to take care of him. Why would he need to buy his own car, when he could always drive hers? Why did he need to put gas in the car when, every time he used it, the supply was magically replenished?

Why would he get his own place when he could live rent free? (In his mind, she was already paying her rent, so it wasn't like it cost her more for him to live there.) She led him down this road, and it wasn't until she got stuck on it that she realized this was not the direction she wanted to go.

Paying for almost all of their shared expenses took a huge bite out of her paycheck. The more David borrowed her car, the less time he seemed to be at home spending time with her (which was what she really wanted most of all). Also, he was always so busy ranting and raving about his problems that by the time she got a word in, he had moved on to the next topic. He seemed uninterested in hearing about her day. She was feeling trapped in this cycle of her world revolving around him. She still wanted to be in a relationship with him, but she was caught between wanting him to depend on her (and stay with her) and feeling overwhelmed by his dependence on her.

In the end David was unwilling to share the practical and financial responsibilities of their household. Jenn sacrificed so much to take care of him, and he left her anyway. His interest in her was less about liking her than about enjoying being mothered by her. He didn't want a relationship, he wanted all the benefits he had when he lived at home with his parents.

Why It Matters

If you are Ms. Mom, I want you to remain the wonderful, supportive, and helpful person that you are—but without losing yourself or forfeiting your rights to be loved as much as you love and care for the man in your life. It's good to be giving, but it's bad to get mistyped as a woman on whom a man can dump all of his problems. That being said, let's take a look at some of the more significant disadvantages to being mistyped as Ms. Mom. If you are Ms. Mom, what are the negative consequences?

• **Your emotional needs and relationship needs don't get met.** When you are singularly focused on mothering the man you are dating, usually his focus will also be on ensuring that his needs get met. The both of you focus on taking care of him, while neither invests enough, if any, time making sure that you are happy and fulfilled. He is so needy that you both silently agree that all of your energy and attention has to be focused on him. In the meantime, you feel emotionally drained and neglected because you are giving him everything you've got. And you get very little in return, other than the satisfaction of having helped him, and you can't live on that alone. If you don't love and value yourself, how will he learn to love and value you? You have to take care of your own needs to have the strength and ability to take care of someone else's.

• **You lose focus on yourself and your life goals.** One reason you may be so busy focusing on your man is that it keeps the attention off yourself. If you have certain life goals that you are struggling with like weight loss, changing jobs, going back to school, or even making new friends, throwing yourself and all your attention into solving a man's problems can be a wanted distraction from solving your own. With your help he may be moving ahead in life, but you're not. You may have a history of choosing to put yourself and your needs second to a boyfriend's. If that is the case, now is the time to change that. You have to give yourself loving attention if you are to be happy and healthy, and if you expect to have a happy and healthy relationship.

♦ **You feel angry, resentful, used, and unappreciated.** When you start giving a man everything he wants and needs, especially without being in a long-term committed relationship, you invite him to take advantage of you. Eventually you get tired of giving and not receiving, and you feel angry and resentful. When you've had enough of giving, or he gets tired of taking and the relationship ends, you feel disappointed, used, and unappreciated. You will find it hard to understand why he wouldn't reciprocate your love and support when you have been so wonderful to him. When it's over, you end up feeling even worse about yourself, which increases the chances that you will remain mistyped as Ms. Mom and fall back into the same trap.

♦ **You feel responsible for something beyond your control.** Believing you can change someone else is a huge burden. You feel personally responsible for what happens to them, so you try to control what happens in your life *and* theirs. When things don't work out in your man's life, you feel guilty and responsible for not doing even more to help. And the more you convince him that it is your responsibility to solve his problems, the more he will blame you for his lack of success.

MOVING FORWARD

You will have to think deeply on how to transform your life so that you stop throwing yourself and all of your resources (financial, emotional, practical) into someone else. (More on how to do this will come a little later in the chapter.) The man you are dating needs to be as focused on you as you are on him. You have to stop believing that you are responsible for your boyfriend's problems and that it is your role to mother him. That belief leads you to attract the type of man who needs a mother, not a girlfriend.

JUST HER TYPE

If you are Ms. Mom, because you are such a selfless giver, you will often attract men who are unhappy and want your help. So you need to be mindful of your vulnerability to these types of men:

Mr. Needy. Since you enjoy being a caretaker and doing things for others, you and Mr. Needy are quite naturally drawn to each other. But stay away. Eventually the lack of reciprocity in your relationship will lead you to resent him, and most likely your relationship will end. You can't go around rescuing men like you might a lost puppy. I know they both look so cute and innocent, but when you rescue a man who is like a lost little puppy, you could end up housing, feeding, and cleaning up after him just like you would Fido.

Mr. Under Construction. Sometimes you meet a man who is really nice but simply doesn't have his stuff together. If he is used to getting by through borrowing money, paying bills late or not at all, and never finishing what he starts, you are hooking up with someone who is going to bring those same values to your relationship. He'll expect you to pick up where he leaves off. Because you don't like to see someone struggling and you feel good when you help others, you step in to help, and now his responsibilities become yours. How are you going to take care of yourself when you are busy taking care of him? Let him get himself together first. You can't expect him to be able to handle the responsibility of taking care of you until he can be responsible enough to take care of himself.

Mr. Unhappily Married. Sometimes you are attracted to a man because you want to fix what he is presenting as his broken little heart. Remember, he is "unhappily" married (though he stays married, right?), so the Ms. Mom in you is all too eager to jump in to solve his problems. He makes his wife sound like a cold-hearted snake who won't be affectionate or have sex with him, and you come to the rescue with all the good loving a man could want. He runs the "poor me" game on you because he can tell you are the type of woman who will work hard to make him happy and hope he will leave his wife for you. But he needs you to believe that fantasy, otherwise you wouldn't cooperate. He can have his cake and eat it too, with a wife and a stable home life and a great girlfriend on the side. Resist the urge to believe that he is broken (if his relationship were that bad, he would leave it), that it is your job to mother him, and that your reward for mothering him back to romantic health will be to win his heart. Don't take the bait!

Mr. Addict. Being an addict makes him appear so needy and vulnerable that a woman like you can't resist wanting to step in and help. But his addictions are more powerful than your love. You can't allow yourself to believe that you can love him out of his addictions, or that your love is strong enough to break his addictions. This is a battle that only he can fight. Dating someone with an addiction is very difficult. For you it's even harder because you have to deal with wanting to control something that you have no control over. You will frustrate him by trying to change him into something he is not ready to be, and you will frustrate yourself, especially when you discover that he is unwilling to change and is unappreciative of your efforts.

The Doctor Is In

Nikki wrote to me for advice at my online advice column, Ask Dr. Michelle (www.drmichelle.com). From her letter, she sounds like a classic Ms. Mom:

> DEAR DR. MICHELLE,
>
> I have been dating this man off and on for about two months. I really like him, and I want to be with him. I cook for him, do his laundry, buy him nice clothes, and other things. He is nice to me too, but sometimes he

just disappears for days without calling. He says he doesn't want a commitment even though he knows that I do. He keeps promising to go back to school or get a regular job. I want to be with him, but he likes to go out and party, and I am the type who likes to stay at home. I went around to local schools to get a list of classes for him and even offered to help him study and loan him the money if he needed it for school. What can I do to get him to be more interested in changing his life? How do I get him to realize what a great woman I am for him?

NIKKI

DEAR NIKKI,

Instead of trying to change someone into the type of man you are looking for, you need to find someone who already has the qualities and lifestyle you need in a mate. You cannot ignore the fact that the man you're dating doesn't have what you need. He won't change into what you need after you start working your "magic" on him. If he isn't already offering you the support and interest you could reasonably expect from someone at this stage in your relationship, you need to think twice about putting any more of yourself (your heart, your mind, your body, your time) out there on the line. Women are taught that this is the way to "catch" a man. Cook him good food, make him feel like he's in charge, and most important, give him the best sex ever. And if you do all of that then you'll get what you want. Wrong! You have to stop acting like his mama and start acting like his partner. He's never going to get off of his butt and act like a man as long as you keep treating him like a boy.

You simply must have balance in your life. When you need an intimate connection or relationship, you may be too willing to do much more than you should, in hopes that you can either make this man "the one" or at least speed up the process of building the relationship. Women open their homes, wallets, and legs in hopes that this will finally be it—the right time, and the right one. But if he can't see what a wonderful and giving person you are, then he isn't the one for you. And why commit yourself to someone who doesn't think you are as great as you are? You can't rush a relationship, and you can't change another person. If you force it, you will waste your precious emotional, spiritual, and material resources, and in the long run you may find yourself back where you started—except with a few more bumps and bruises, like ruined credit, fewer friends, and a broken heart. Don't just give yourself away.

How You Became Mistyped
as Ms. Mom

You may be wondering, How did I become Ms. Mom? Here are some experiences that may have influenced you growing up:

+ Your mother was a Ms. Mom, and you watched and learned from her that when a woman is in a relationship, she should do any and everything a man needs done, even at her own expense.
+ You were Ms. Mom around your house growing up, being told (or offering) to do things for the men in

your house (father, brothers, or another needy family member).

♦ Your friends were Ms. Moms and shared with you the things that they did for their boyfriends. This led you to believe that you had to do those same kinds of things, otherwise you wouldn't have a boyfriend.

♦ Your boyfriends led you to feel you needed to be Ms. Mom to be in a relationship with them. They convinced you that other women were doing certain things for them that you did not.

♦ You observed many real-life Ms. Moms as well as television and movie portrayals of women who went far out of their way to do things for the men they were dating. (How many movies or soap operas have you watched where the woman did some extraordinary things for the man and it won over his heart?)

The younger you were when any of these things might have happened, the more likely you were to believe that this was not a unique situation that related only to that particular man and time, but instead was how all men were and how all relationships worked. Sit back and think for a while about how you may have been encouraged to become Ms. Mom. This will help you recognize what influences you need to resist and steer away from in the future. Taking care of people and caring about their problems is a very positive thing. You are still an important person yourself, however, and you deserve the opportunity to be cared for and supported. Your dating challenge is not to change from being a loving and caring person toward others, but to learn to allow others to care for you, and to ask for the love and care that you need.

A MS. TYPED MAKEOVER: FROM MS. MOM TO MS. NO MAMA'S BOYS

If you are ready to say goodbye to Ms. Mom, you will have to learn how to shift your focus from man-care to self-care. I don't mean you should become selfish. Rather, you need to treat yourself well and demand that your partner take care of your needs. It is very thoughtful to help the man you love, but you need to stop doing that in excess. It cripples his ability to take care of himself, and it gives him permission to take attention away from you. Take this opportunity to give your vital resources like time, money, and attention to yourself, so that you can improve your life. Look within to determine why you are so willing to give it all away to someone else instead of saving some for yourself (which you deserve!). Here are some things you can do differently, going forward, to help you evolve from Ms. Mom to Ms. No Mama's Boys:

Wait patiently while your man resolves his own problems. The needy men you date usually don't take care of themselves or are happy to let you take care of them. Instead of immediately jumping in to take over a man's life and problems, assume he can handle them himself. Give him the time and opportunity to step up and resolve things on his own. Stop trying to solve his problems, and be patient enough to wait for him to get it together. You have to stop trying to break his fall and allow him to make mistakes or even fail at something.

You also need to take small steps in censoring your natural desire to help a man. Often you see a need and step up to take responsibility for improving his situation. Start catching yourself in the act of involving yourself in his problems or coming to his rescue. When you are about to interfere or intervene, stop and ask yourself if this is something that needs to be done at all, and if so, is it something you should do for him or he should do for himself? Don't steal from him the sense of pride and accomplishment he can experience when he takes care of himself.

Be more assertive about your wants and needs. Either ask for or tell him what you need. This includes feeling comfortable saying no to some of the things he asks you to do. It's never too late to speak up and say that you no longer feel comfortable with how things are going or to say that you need some help or attention. You have power over what is happening. If you are dating someone who is selfish, then you probably can't change that. But you might be dating someone who isn't selfish, but whom you have taught and rewarded for behaving selfishly. By encouraging him to take and not give, you have set the tone. If you date someone and allow him to use you and your resources without giving back, then you are just as responsible for your situation as he is. You can't allow your desire to be supportive or a caregiver to override your right to

MS. MOM

143

be supported and loved. Speak up early, and you will be much happier in the long run. Remain silent, and it will eventually undermine you and your relationships.

Don't act like a wife too soon. Much of the problem solving you take on requires a lot more involvement than you should probably have in the life of someone you are dating. If you were married to the man, then pooling your resources and doing certain things to take care of each other would be expected. But when you are only dating someone (and may eventually be dating someone else), you shouldn't be so quick to act like a wife or a mother. If he can't stand on his own two feet without your help, do you really want him to become your husband? Don't rush to do all the duties of a wife. If and when you get married, you'll have lots of time to cook, clean, and help pay his bills.

Stop dating needy and irresponsible men. This may be hard for you because you are drawn to each other. Now that you know the personal characteristics of the type of man whom you attract but should avoid, you are fully equipped with the information you need to recognize when things are becoming unhealthy. When headed in that direction, you either have to quickly change the tone and direction of the relationship (you give, he takes), or assume that you can't change him into the right man for you and stop pursuing the relationship.

Don't panic or give in if your man gets upset when you stop mothering him. When you start to assert yourself and work more on your own priorities, your man will notice and may respond by acting even needier or by becoming upset and accusing you of not caring about him. Don't panic and go back to the old Ms. Mom. Calmly explain that your feelings for him haven't changed, but that you have certain things you need to do, so he will have to resolve the issue at hand on his own.

Practice what to say to your man about your needs. Eventually you are going to have to assert yourself in your dating relationship and ask for what you want and need; if you aren't entirely comfortable doing that yet, you can practice it first. You can do it alone or with a friend. Rehearse and go over what you want to say to your boyfriend. Let your friend pretend to be him, or rehearse it in your head. This is one method for relieving any anxiety or nervousness you might feel about learning to speak up and say no. Another way to practice is to address a situation in your life with someone other than your boyfriend, and start by changing how you behave with that person. For example, let's say the person is your best friend who you always do things for, so much so that you barely get your own daily tasks accomplished. Approach your friend and tell her how you feel, what you need, and what your goals are going forward. The more you practice and get into the habit of telling people what you need and making choices that benefit you, the easier it will become. Start with something small, and then move up to those more difficult conversations about the things you value most.

The problem solving should go both ways. Being in a relationship should make you both better people. He may not do the same kind of problem solving for you as you do for him, but if you are spending all your time minding his business, chances are that you aren't spending any time minding your own. In that case, being in the relationship certainly isn't making either of you better people, because neither of you is taking care of *your* needs. You probably think that taking care of him is making him a better person, but it isn't. The things you do might make his life look better on the surface, but they aren't making him a better man. You can help him become a better man by allowing him the chance to experience the pride of taking care of himself.

If he can't meet your needs, move on. Your desire to be in a relationship can drive you to work hard, investing both time and energy, on changing the man you are dating into the kind of man you need to be dating. But instead of trying to change him, you might need to end the relationship altogether and seek out a more compatible partner. You have to get used to the idea that until you are ready to marry, you are supposed to keep dating different men until you find one worth settling down with, not try to settle down with every man you date. If he can't meet your needs, move on.

Don't be afraid to be vulnerable. Sometimes putting up such a strong front gives men the false impression that you are always okay and that you don't need help or support. While you are busy trying to rescue him, neither one of you may realize that you are drowning too! Set the tone that lets him know that you need and expect his support. Don't try to mask your feelings and needs, so that he assumes you are doing okay when you aren't. Allow your true self to shine through. Let it be known when you need a hand or a shoulder to lean on, so that he can have the opportunity to do something to support you. If you always act like you don't need any help, he may never offer any.

Be more assertive in your nondating relationships. Many of the challenges you face in dating come up in other relationships as well. Your selfless, giving nature can lead you to the same frustrations with friends and family as it does with men. When you stop taking on other people's problems and learn to ask for what you need in your friendships, it will become easier for you to do the same when dating.

Spend more time working on your goals. When it comes to making changes, most people are quick to jump on somebody else's bandwagon, telling them what to do and how to do it. Since you are now taking responsibility for your own life instead of everyone else's, you will put as much energy into improving and changing yourself for the better as you have put into anyone you have dated. Many women manage to help their partners do everything from getting off drugs to graduating college, so if you can do that much for someone else, I want to see you make that much of a commitment to yourself, starting today! Start by loving yourself as much as you are willing to love the man you are dating. Sometimes it's easier to put off working toward your own difficult personal goals and focus on the items on his task list. Instead, you need to make sure that you are living up to your own personal potential. Stay focused on your goals. If you aren't sure what your priorities are in life or if you don't have any goals, then start by setting some goals for yourself. (See the Ms. Typed Makeover Kit.) Then spend time discovering who you are and what you like outside of your relationship.

Ms. Anaconda

What She Looks Like

◆ Fears being left alone or being betrayed, so she is "all over" a man to keep him around and in line.

◆ Is so afraid of losing her relationship that she is constantly taking a man's temperature to find out what he is feeling, thinking, and desiring at every moment.

◆ Hopes that her hyper-attention to a relationship will prevent problems from arising. She doesn't realize she is causing the problems!

◆ Feels lonely or isolated, which places additional pressure on a man. She expects a relationship to be her whole world.

◆ Acts very jealous. She is possessive and often accuses men of cheating. She needs constant reassurance that a man is still interested in her.

◆ Feels uncomfortable when she is not with her man and gets very upset when she detects any change in his behavior or apparent distance between them.

◆ Has many other names, including Ms. Melodramatic and Ms. Manipulator.

An anaconda isn't a poisonous snake—it kills its prey by wrapping itself around it until it suffocates. Ms. Anaconda does the exact same thing to her men. She is so paranoid and anxious about a man leaving her or betraying her that she thinks she can prevent it from happening by holding on tightly. The more she chases or holds on to a man, the faster he runs away. What she doesn't realize is that holding him so tight smothers him. She expects to be betrayed, so she treats him like he can't be trusted. He responds by pulling away in anger, and her fears are confirmed. Smothering her man makes him want to leave her, which is exactly what she was trying to prevent in the first place. Relationships can't survive under that type of pressure, but she still hopes for the best. She believes that as long as she is with him and knows where he is, or what he is doing at all times, she can prevent him from hurting her.

THE ROLES SHE PLAYS

There are several Ms. Anaconda roles that women play in dating relationships, including:

◆ **Ms. Melodramatic.** She overreacts to a situation as if it were the end of the world and the relationship. Even when there is no fire, she won't believe it.

◆ **Ms. Manipulator.** She fakes illnesses or exaggerates problems to get more attention from her man. She will stop at nothing to keep her man interested and invested.

◆ **Ms. Friendship Killer.** She smothers her man and keeps him from his friends, which only makes him resent her and try to pull away.

◆ **Ms. Nurse.** She is checking in on her man every minute of the day to see how he is feeling about her and their relationship. If he sounds like his temperature is cooling off, she jumps right in, trying to bring the fire back into the relationship.

Just Like You ....
Ms. Anaconda has some of the same concerns about betrayal and abandonment as Ms. Independent and Ms. Bag Lady, so be sure to check out their profiles as well.

Janelle's Story

Janelle and Charles were so close that at times they appeared inseparable. Janelle did just about everything with Charles and felt lost without him. When they were apart, they kept in close contact by phone, e-mail, and texting. Sadly, Charles's grandfather became ill, and his condition took a turn for the worse. On top of that, his mom was having a very difficult time with the situation, and his family wasn't seeing eye to eye on how to handle his grandfather's health or his estate. Charles needed to go home in a hurry to see his grandfather and to help manage these very sensitive family issues. Janelle offered to take off from work to join him, but because he was planning to leave immediately, he suggested she stay home and keep working until he knew more about what was going on. That way if his grandfather passed away, she could join him later, or maybe his grandfather would improve and he would be back soon. Either way, he couldn't wait, he needed to hurry up and get home. She could join him soon, after he had a chance to deal with his family.

When he told Janelle his suggested plan, she lost it. She cried and insisted that if they were close and he really loved her, she should come with him. He told her it had nothing to do with her and that he simply needed to handle his family business sooner rather than later. They could make a plan for her to come sometime after he got there. Janelle was still inconsolable. She was so upset that she accused Charles of planning to see his ex-girlfriend while he was home—she must be the reason he didn't want her to come along. Nothing Charles could say would calm her down. He eventually broke down and told her it was fine if she wanted to come with him now, but he had to leave right away. That still didn't satisfy her. Now she was unhappy because she thought he had invited her only because she'd insisted. She told him he might as well just go and be with his ex.

So What?

If Charles and Janelle were really that close, shouldn't she have been by his side at a time like this? The issue here is not whether she should have been invited. Charles simply asked her to wait until he got there, to figure out if and when she should come. The obvious problem here is her insecure and stressful overreaction to the situation. As if Charles wasn't stressed enough by his grandfather possibly passing away and his family feuding over the situation, Janelle decided to let her insecurities get the best of her, and she fought with him and accused him of cheating on her. At a time when he needed her to be calm, she was anything but. This is the kind of behavior that drives both parties crazy. Men hate it when women behave irrationally and become overly emotional about issues that don't call for that level of anxiety. More important, Janelle sent herself on a totally unnecessary emotional roller coaster, questioning Charles's love for her and throwing out wild accusations.

Did she really believe what she was saying? Yes and no. Up until that moment she had no legitimate concerns about Charles's love or fidelity. But as soon as he talked about having to leave and be away from her, even for a short time, she panicked and all rational thought left her. Instead of remem-

153

bering how great everything was and assuming it would continue to be that way, she let Charles's trip trigger her fears and insecurities. She believed his leaving meant something about his feelings for her (where it's obvious to us that the two had nothing to do with each other). In the middle of her relationship panic attack, she convinced herself that this decision must be a negative reflection of his feelings for her, that he must not care for her, or he must care for someone else. She put her worst fears out there for him to refute. Then no matter what he said, she didn't listen and didn't believe him anyway. A situation like this was bad for them individually and for their relationship.

Instead of panicking and assuming the worst, Janelle should have trusted Charles to tell the truth and do what he said he would. She had absolutely no evidence to support, or reason to believe, that things were going downhill between them. Her fears brought on the fighting and negative feelings. As long as she continued to act as if she expected the worst, her worst fears would come true. Her irrational behavior would push Charles away.

Why It Matters

If you have been mistyped as Ms. Anaconda, what are the negative consequences when your fear causes you to keep such a tight hold on your man?

You walk on eggshells. As Ms. Anaconda, you are always waiting for the other shoe to drop. You constantly live in fear, waiting for your man to do something to hurt or disappoint you. Regardless of how good things seem, you still worry that your relationship is doomed to fail. As a result you walk on eggshells, which is exhausting to you personally, and it drains the life out of your relationship.

You are too emotionally dependent on men. Too much of your time and energy are wrapped up in men and relationships. You never stop thinking about either. You depend on a man to make your life complete. How you feel about yourself and your life is measured by how you think things are going in your relationship. You are happy when you believe things are going well and sad over the slightest hint of change or momentary distance from a man.

Your emotions are too easily triggered. Because you live with such anxiety, your emotions are triggered by the smallest events. If at any time a man seems bored or acts distant or distracted, your anxiety is set into motion. If he makes the mistake of turning away from you to pay attention to what someone else is saying, it makes you feel rejected. You can't survive watching your man with a magnifying glass. Analyzing his every word and behavior to determine if it means that he is planning to leave you will only drive you crazy.

You get caught up in a cycle of fear. You live in a constant state of fear of the unknown. You are convinced that at some point your relationship will end. You live through every day as if the end might come today. At the first sign that things might be changing, you act as if they have already changed for the worse and that the relationship is over. You are filled with anxiety as you wait to see if you are right, and then you are filled with sadness when you assume it must be the beginning of the end. Then at some point you discover that the relationship is not over, which fills you with anger—at him for doing whatever he did that triggered your fear, and at yourself for being so caught up in him that you can't control your feelings. This process repeats itself over and over. Acting as if something negative is going to happen brings you nothing more than unhappiness and unpleasant experiences.

You neglect yourself. When you are so focused on the man you are dating and the state of your relationship, you have very little time to focus on yourself. As a result, you may be allowing your relationship to become your entire world, and you may be ignoring other important areas of your life, like your physical and mental health, career, finances, family, and friendships. This type of neglect—ignoring everything and everyone because all your time and attention is focused on the man you are dating—can have a huge negative impact on your life. When the relationship ends, it may not be so easy to pick up the pieces and put things back together. So you should make sure you take care of yourself and your life while you're dating.

THE DOCTOR IS IN

Amber wrote to me for my advice at my online advice column, Ask Dr. Michelle. Based on what she wrote, she sounds like Ms. Anaconda:

DEAR DR. MICHELLE,

I have been dating my boyfriend for a year. My entire life revolves around him. I spend all of my time with him, and I miss him when we are apart. He keeps telling me that he needs some space and that he wants to spend more time with his friends, but I think we should all be able to hang out together. He said that some-times men just want to hang out with other men and I should get some friends of my own to hang out with. Whenever I try to hang out with a friend, I end up spending the entire time calling or texting him on the phone to find out where he is and what he is doing. I usually get so worried about what he might be doing without me that I come home early. Sometimes I think he might be cheating with other girls or just having fun without me. How can I learn to let go and not become so obsessed with him that I can't enjoy being away from him for even one hour?

THANKS, AMBER

DEAR AMBER,

It's good to hear that you realize when you are being too overbearing and are smothering your boyfriend and your relationship. You are going to have to slowly start doing things without your boyfriend. I know you want to be with him all the time, but you have to trust me when I say that all couples need some time apart. You probably already think you spend enough time apart, but you don't want to wait until your life has fallen apart from neglect, and your boyfriend gets fed up with your behavior, to decide to change. Now is a great time to work on bringing balance back into your life and to let go of the fear of being away from your boyfriend.

You can start by allowing yourself and your boyfriend some alone time to do things you like to do, either by yourselves or with your own friends. If you almost never go out with your friends or spend time alone, you need to learn to feel comfortable doing so. It just takes a little practice. Over time you will discover that nothing bad is going to happen while you are apart, and you will feel more relaxed during that time. In the beginning you may stay in close communication by phone, but you will eventually become comfortable being away from him and letting some time go by without a call.

It is very important that you not "lose yourself" in your relationship. Before you had a boyfriend, you must have had a life of your own where you spent time doing different things and hanging out with other people. Obviously, being in a relationship changes that some-what, but don't drop all your old goals and priorities in order to follow your boyfriend around everywhere he goes. Many women make the mistake of thinking that doing everything with their boyfriend, and no one else, is good or better for their relationship. However, going to that extreme puts your relationship out of balance and can make him feel smothered. You cannot live in fear that your relationship will end if you don't spend every waking moment with your man. You think always being around will prevent a problem when it is more likely to cause a problem.

Don't be afraid that he is going to have so much fun without you that he will want to spend even less time with you or break up. Some healthy time apart is most likely going to make him miss you and be more excited to see you when you meet again. Start slowly by getting back in touch with your friends and family. Then try to schedule something like a movie or a lunch date. If you have been neglecting other areas of your life, maybe you need to spend the time away from your man studying, paying bills, or hitting the gym. The more time you spend apart without the sky falling, the more comfortable you will become loosening your grip on him. You may be surprised to discover that a little space between you motivates him to chase after you. Now wouldn't that be fun?

Just Her Type

If you are Ms. Anaconda, you often attract the types of men who are hard to hold on to and who bring out your fear of being betrayed or left alone. You are very sensitive to being abandoned and therefore are vulnerable to:

Mr. Player. Mr. Player will always keep you walking on eggshells because his objective is to date as many different women as possible. You will never feel safe or confident with him because he gains his confidence from having many women around him, whereas you gain confidence from having the commitment of one man. He will always have you rightfully worrying that he is seeing someone else. Depending on how many other women he has lined up, one minute he might be all over you and the next he could treat you like you have no relationship history together.

Mr. Money. Mr. Money has a lot of what most women are looking for in a man. His success and money enable him to show women the time of their lives. When you are with him, you worry that he is going to want someone bigger and better than you. You figure that with what he has to offer, he can have any woman he wants, so you worry that this ideal woman won't be you. That, coupled with the women who are already coming after him, keeps you from getting a good night's sleep.

Mr. Pleasure Principle. The pleasure this man brings you quite naturally makes you want to squeeze him tighter, but his sole focus on sex makes him hard to hold on to. You are vulnerable to him because, as much as you might enjoy dating him, he is mainly into having a good time. And you will always worry that there is someone else who is doing it better than you are. That fear will drive you both crazy and eventually ruin even your sexual relationship.

How You Became Mistyped
as Ms. Anaconda

You may be wondering how you became Ms. Anaconda and why you are so fearful of being abandoned, betrayed, or rejected. It can start when you are very young. Here are some experiences that may have influenced you:

◆ Your home environment was unstable, and you felt that no one was really available and accessible to care for you. This left you feeling very anxious and alone.

160

- Your parents spent a lot of time apart from you or they divorced, and it left you feeling vulnerable and insecure. This could cause you to seek the stability and consistent support from a man that you never received in your home.
- Your home life was very stable and you felt well cared for. So as an adult you feel exposed without someone there who promises to guide you and care for you in the way that your parents once did.
- Your mother was a Ms. Anaconda, and you watched her keep men very close to her for fear that they might leave her.
- Your friends were Ms. Anacondas, and you sat around analyzing everything your boyfriends said, unintentionally encouraging each other to become more worried and fearful.
- You trusted the men you dated to spend time apart from you, only to discover later that they were cheating on you.

A MS. TYPED MAKEOVER: FROM MS. ANACONDA TO MS. LOOSENED UP

If you are tired of being mistyped as Ms. Anaconda, you need to learn to be comfortable in your world independent of a man. If that is your greatest fear, you need to conquer it, so that dating relationships don't hold your emotions hostage. You need to be confident that if you are in a happy dating

161

relationship, your man will not be constantly on the verge of leaving you. And if he did, you would survive and someday find a new love that could be even stronger. You can't give away all your confidence and strength in exchange for fear. You can't worry every day. You need to know that things aren't going to fall apart if you take a break from your constant worry.

Over time you will grow and evolve into a woman who is less fearful and more comfortable in her relationships. It may seem far off because you are used to living with constant anxiety, but it's not. You simply have to be patient and allow yourself the opportunity to grow. Creating new healthy habits takes hard work. Here are some things to assist you with your awesome transformation:

Avoid clinging or overreacting. There are quite naturally going to be disappointments throughout any relationship, and you have to be careful that you don't run yourself ragged overreacting to each and every one of them. It might be a canceled date, an unreturned phone call, or a smaller gift than expected. Don't let something that doesn't signal the end of your dating relationship send you into a tailspin. If he doesn't call you on your birthday, then you have cause for concern, but if he takes you out to dinner and forgets to pull out your chair and make a special birthday toast, don't assume that means he doesn't love you anymore.

Resist the urge to become jealous. Sadly, men more often than women have rich and full lives outside their dating relationships. They have hobbies and friends and stay busy living. Women, on the other hand, so frequently put men first that they lose out on the rest of what life has to offer. They "settle" for friends and hobbies to pass the time when men aren't available, then ditch both when their men are available again.

There's nothing wrong with him spending some time away from you, blowing off steam with his friends, and then coming to see you after having the opportunity to miss you. Some Ms. Anacondas even get jealous when their man is looking at another woman in a movie they are watching together. Come on, ladies! You have got to learn to relax. Don't let fictional characters, unattainable celebrities, and sports championships get you down. You are going to squeeze all the fun out of life if you become jealous of everything your man does that doesn't include you. Accept that it is a part of the balance that he needs in his life, and work on adding that balance to your life as well.

Stop the stalking. It is possible to squeeze the life out of a dating relationship. And if you don't lighten up, you will do it. One of the worst ways of smothering your man is to stalk him. You can't follow him everywhere and keep showing up wherever he is planning to be. If you weren't invited, don't force yourself into the situation. If he doesn't want you around, your challenge isn't to follow him; it's to find a man who wants you to spend more time with him. By stalking, I also mean tracking him down by phone wherever he goes. You can't live "virtually" by cell phone through every life experience with him. When you aren't doing something together, then do your own thing. You can share your experiences when you're both finished.

Loosen up. If being Ms. Anaconda is really an indication of your overall anxiety level, then you want to work on loosening up in all aspects of your life. You probably worry too much about everything! You may become overbearing as a way to try to regain some control. You can't usually control another adult, especially a man, only yourself. Instead of trying to be in control, why not learn to relax and enjoy life as it comes? If you don't know how to relax, then you should try meditation, prayer, yoga, working out, or taking long walks. Choose physical and psychological activities that can take your mind off of your worries and bring you back into the here and now.

Resolve issues of distrust. If you were mistreated before, you might be holding on too tight in fear of the same thing happening again. Maybe your old boyfriend cheated on you, so you figure if you follow this new one everywhere and keep tabs on him at all times, he won't have a chance to do it too. And even if he tried, you think you would be able to catch him. Worrying about this is no way to live. Instead of anticipating something good, you are living in expectation of something bad happening all the time, which only leads to misery— yours. No matter what happened in the past to make you feel you can't trust men, you can heal from it and live a more relaxed and trusting life. Don't be afraid to seek the help of a mental health professional, if needed, to help support you in healing past hurts.

Don't take advice from other Ms. Anacondas. Part of breaking your habit of being overbearing might involve moving away from friendships with other Ms. Anacondas. Just as with any other bad habit, if you are trying to break it but are hanging around others who aren't, their behavior might sabotage your success. If you want to stop smothering your man and your relationship, you can't take advice from other women who are doing all the things you're trying to stop doing. Their perspective on dating is skewed toward being controlling, so following their lead is only bound to get you into more trouble. Instead, try to identify other women who are in healthier relationships and spend some social time with them. That way you can learn more about healthy relationships by talking and observing their lives and interactions with their mates.

Develop relationships outside romance. Every relationship needs balance, and one way to get it is to make sure that you have relationships with people besides your boyfriend. He cannot be your whole world because you will overburden and smother him with all your attention. Some of the entertainment and support you need should come from friends, family, acquaintances, or coworkers. These other relationships provide you with a broader perspective on issues, new experiences, and new opportunities to enjoy life. Having these relationships is the proof you need that there is life and happiness outside of a dating relationship; they also give you the downtime you both need away from each other. When you spend time apart, you have the opportunity to miss each other—and get excited when you see each other again. Try it!

Make a life of your own. Don't stop at just making new friends—make sure that you have a life of your own outside your relationship with your boyfriend. The less life you have, the tighter you are going to squeeze. If this describes you, then things are going to have to change around here! Make changes in all the areas of your life where you know things could be better. This could include your health, career, finances, community, spirituality, education, family, friendship, and hobbies. (See the Ms. Typed Makeover Kit.) When you are working on getting and keeping these things in order, you will have less time to worry about what your man is doing. Once you get a life, you will be much happier and more satisfied with yourself, and you'll improve your relationship. It might seem scary at first to be doing things on your own, but you can do it!

Ms. Independent

What She Looks Like

♦ Fears intimacy and commitment. Allowing herself to fall in love would make her vulnerable to being rejected or left alone.

♦ Acts defensive and hides behind her work, family, weight, and anything else to avoid the vulnerability of a relationship.

♦ Doesn't trust men. She expects all men to eventually disappoint and hurt her.

♦ Is suspicious and responds negatively when a man tries to be nice, affectionate, or loving.

- Often has negative beliefs about herself and feels unlovable.

- Has many other names, including Ms. Career Woman, Ms. Commitment Phobic, and Ms. Loner.

Ms. Independent avoids dating relationships so she can avoid being hurt. She doesn't trust men. She expects them to either disappoint or betray her by cheating or abandoning her. She's been hurt and let down by men in the past, and she can't bring herself to lower her guard and risk the pain again. Deep down she believes she is flawed and that that is the reason men leave. Even when men try to prove to her that she is a wonderful and lovable person—by acting nice, considerate, and loving toward her—she doubts them. She often overlooks the positive, only seeing the negative, both in herself and in the men she dates. As much as she secretly wants a relationship, her negativity undermines everything.

THE ROLES SHE PLAYS

There are several Ms. Independent roles that women play to avoid relationships, including:

- **Ms. Career Woman.** She is so focused on her career and personal development that she leaves romance off of her list of priorities. She doesn't want to risk a dating disappointment having a negative affect on her professional success.

♦ **Ms. Commitment Phobic.** She is afraid of getting hurt in relationships so she avoids intimacy and commitment in hopes that her heart will be safe. When she does date, she doesn't allow anyone to get close to her.

♦ **Ms. Busy Body.** She avoids relationships by staying too busy to date. She is always working long hours, starting new projects, being a good Samaritan, and filling her days and nights with obligations that keep herself out of the dating scene.

♦ **Ms. Man Hater.** She's been hurt so many times that she assumes all men are dogs. She doesn't trust or want anything to do with them, so she doesn't date.

♦ **Ms. Loner.** In an attempt to avoid dating, she becomes a loner and avoids social situations where she would be approached by men or encouraged by her friends to mingle or flirt. She allows her fear to obstruct her opportunities to be more social. She ends up alienated from everyone.

Just Like You ....
Ms. Bag Lady and Ms. Anaconda can also be very afraid of being hurt or abandoned by the men they are dating. Be sure to read about both of them.

NICOLE'S STORY

Nicole was your typical workaholic. At the top of her game at work, she had not been on a date in months. She'd had a serious boyfriend Jason, a former classmate in business school, several years back. But since then there weren't any dates. She had desperately wanted to get married and start a family, but Jason kept saying he wasn't ready. Because of his inability to commit to her, they grew apart and eventually broke up. Six months later one of Nicole's friends called to tell her that Jason was engaged and his fiancée was pregnant. She hit the ceiling, and then she hit the floor—she was devastated. Had he been cheating with this woman while they were still together? What happened? Worst of all, she couldn't believe he was willing to marry someone else when he hadn't been willing to marry her. She felt completely betrayed. After all, she'd invested a lot of time and sacrificed quite a bit for him and their relationship.

When it came to men, this experience was the final straw for Nicole. Each one seemed to have some excuse for why it was okay to break her heart. And she felt like she couldn't take it anymore. After hearing Jason's news, she knew how to cope only by throwing herself into work. She hoped that by staying busy, she would forget sooner. After all, she was a vice president at a large international bank, and she had a lot going for her. Well known and widely respected in the organization, Nicole was expected to continue to rise even perhaps to become the head of her entire global division within five to ten years. Years after Jason she was so immersed in her job that she was in fact at the top of the list of people expected to next head up the global division.

After Jason became ancient history, Nicole's friends always tried to hook her up with someone. But she was unimpressed with their choices. She felt that few men, if any, were worth putting her work down, in order to pick them up.

So What?

If Nicole was on the fast track to being the head honcho at her bank, why should she have derailed herself for dinner and a movie? She shouldn't have. But she had convinced herself that dating would derail her from her plans—and that was the problem. There are lots of successful women in committed relationships. You *can* have a career and a man. Much as Ms. Mom uses helping her man to avoid helping herself, Ms. Independent sometimes uses her professional life to avoid having a personal life. It is easy to get so wrapped up in work that you spend less and less time on yourself and on nurturing your relationships.

If you haven't had success in the romance department, or you don't believe that there's anyone out there for you anyway, it's easier to take yourself out of the dating game altogether. As long as Nicole works fourteen-hour days, she can keep dating on the back burner and avoid doing it. As much as she loves her job, she needs to be honest with herself. She gives it a lot more time and energy than she should because it has become her whole life. Years ago she wanted marriage and children, but she let her pain take her out of the dating game altogether. She doesn't have to give up her career to have a social life, but she does have to let go of her painful past and be willing to risk falling in love again. She wants to avoid getting hurt, but that means she also avoids falling in love. She can't do both at the same time. Her heartbreak contributed to her becoming mistyped as a workaholic, when in many ways she's using her career as an escape.

Why It Matters

What are the negative consequences of being mistyped and letting the fear of getting hurt keep you from reaching out?

You believe you are unlovable. The longer you go without experiencing love, the more unlovable you feel. Your belief that something about you is incomplete or unlovable probably began long ago. But when you avoid dating, you don't get the opportunity to prove yourself wrong. When you allow someone to love you and you experience it too, you get evidence that your negative thoughts are wrong. But when you hide from love and don't experience it, those false beliefs live on, waiting to be disproved. You can't afford to walk around feeling bad about yourself. There is nothing wrong with you. You are lovable and deserving of love. You just need to take the time to heal from your past hurts. You can learn to trust again and make yourself available to experience love and intimacy.

You live with anxiety and fear about dating. When you avoid men, over time you become even more anxious about what bad things a relationship might bring. You keep building up your fears and negative expectations, so when an opportunity presents itself, you say no way and back off. You have to stop worrying about what's going to happen. We all love and we all get hurt; it is a normal part of life and dating. But without taking a risk, you can't experience the reward. Getting hurt teaches us who and what to avoid or pursue in the future. You will never experience the pleasure of love unless you give dating and relationships a chance.

It's sort of like when you were a kid and you went swimming and the water went up your nose. It hurt so bad, maybe you decided to never put your head under the water again. (I know I did.) And so for a long time you missed out on how much fun the pool or the ocean could be. The more you thought about it, the less you wanted to go anywhere near the water, let alone actually try to swim. And then one day, somehow, you went under the water, and it didn't go up your nose. And in that instant everything changed. You discovered it was possible to enjoy water and swimming without pain. And you realized that all the time you were worried for nothing. Later on I'm sure that tricky water found its way up your nose again and it was uncomfortable. But by that time you had swum successfully so many times without pain that you just shook the feeling off and kept on swimming.

This is an overly simple way to describe my point, but in a nutshell it's what needs to happen to you. The very thing that you are most afraid of doing is the thing you need to do in order to break your fear. Your fear and anxiety about relationships cause you to avoid the joy you could find in them. It keeps you feeling less than others, as you watch everyone else around you falling in love and enjoying companionship.

You become prejudiced. You've been hurt in the past, and that makes you assume that the next man is going to hurt you as the last one did. When you become so distrustful, you judge men harshly and unfairly before you get a chance to know them. You undermine your ability to make a good friend or find someone nice to date, by jumping to wrong conclusions about men based on false assumptions and too little informa-tion. You can't let your past experiences prejudice you against new people. In order to get to know a man's true nature and intentions, you will have to give him an opportunity to prove himself, before you assume that because he is a man, he must be like all the others.

You are suspicious. A successful relationship is built on trust. If you don't have that trust in the man you're dating, you live with constant fear and anxiety of being wronged. When you finally allow someone to enter your life, you are very dis-trustful and suspicious of his intentions. You assume that he is saying and doing positive things as a way to trick or manipu-late you. And you fear that this will result in your getting hurt. You have to accept that all men are not built the same, and see each new relationship as an opportunity for a positive dat-ing experience, despite what you've experienced in the past.

You miss out on the joy of intimacy. One of life's greatest pleasures is the experience of love and intimacy. Love brings people joy. You want to experience that joy, but you are afraid of the possible pain. We take risks in life every day, from the moment we wake up. But this risk has a big payoff. You will be much happier when you find a man you can trust and with whom you can comfortably be yourself. It may not be easy, and you may have to proceed slowly and carefully, but once you find him, you will have the freedom of letting your hair down and the joy of being loved for who you are. Do you really want being Ms. Independent to rob you of that great experience?

JUST HER TYPE

If you are Ms. Independent, you attract men who are also anti-relationship, which makes you vulnerable to:

Mr. Player. You are attracted to Mr. Player because you know he has lots of other women to keep him entertained. When you get scared of getting too close, you can step back, and he will let someone else take your spot. Both of you are so busy running away from each other that you will never get a relationship off the ground. That's good for you, if you are still on the run, but bad if you want to stop, stay, and learn to love. He looks like a good candidate because you know he won't push to get to know you well or on an emotional level. That very thing is what keeps you trapped in your role as Ms. Independent.

Mr. Money. He doesn't have time for a relationship, so when you hang out, he's happy to act like a boyfriend over dinner and during sex. But the rest of the time, his mind is elsewhere. You are vulnerable to him because he is only looking for a little arm candy every once in a while; when you are ready to be more than Ms. Independent, there will be no room here for advancement.

Mr. Pleasure Principle. He will gladly give you sex all day, but a dating relationship will not become part of the deal. I

175

know you think you don't want a relationship. But if and when you change your mind, you want to be dating someone who would at least consider dating you long term. If you get caught up in Mr. Pleasure Principle's sex moves, that's all you will ever get. You will be his booty call girl, even if that identity no longer works for you.

Mr. Unhappily Married. You like Mr. Unhappily Married because he is unavailable for much more than an affair. He can't live with you, and there are many times when he can't see or speak to you. This distance gives you a false sense of being less vulnerable. The relationship is no good for you because it totally restricts your ability to move forward, as you grow more comfortable and at ease with the idea of intimacy and commitment. Even if you eventually get there, he can't meet you there.

Mr. Ex Factor. Mr. Ex Factor is another man you attract because you know you have an escape route. This relationship is not meant to go anywhere. Your ex ends up blocking other opportunities, as hooking up with him keeps you from dating other men. If you keep seeing him and sleeping with him, chances are you still have feelings for him. These feelings get in the way of you developing feelings for a new man in your life. He's not offering a relationship, and he's blocking any potential you have with someone else. Cut him loose, because you need a chance at love!

How You Became Mistyped
as Ms. Independent

If you are wondering how you became mistyped as Ms. Independent, it is probably a combination of experiences—ones that taught you that people are unpredictable and inconsistent. Here are several things you may have experienced that also contributed:

- The men you dated were afraid to be intimate, and their defensive behavior made you feel you should keep your distance.
- You dated men who were mean to you, reinforcing the belief that you couldn't be yourself while dating.
- The men you dated abandoned you, and it left you feeling that attempts at romance were pointless.
- Your parents were together but never really felt comfortable being themselves. You learned how relationships "work" by watching them be distant from, and defensive toward, each other.
- You listened and learned from the women in your family and your friends, who told tales of how men can't be trusted and will all eventually break your heart.
- Your mother was Ms. Independent, and you observed her being distrustful of and distant with your father or the men she dated.
- Your parents didn't offer you enough emotional support and weren't consistently there for you when you needed them. So you grew up feeling that it was you against the world.

Our society doesn't encourage women to become Ms. Independent the way it encourages some of the other types. We don't praise women for being successful and single, and certainly not for avoiding relationships. Chances are, you go against most people's obsession with love and dating because you are genuinely scared of being hurt. You've developed a fear of dating, and you need to get right back on that horse and try again. You want to experience love and intimacy, but trying fills you with so much anxiety and fear that you usually do something to sabotage the relationship. Recognizing what you feel and realizing how you've been acting are the first steps toward change. Don't worry, there is hope for you.

A MS. TYPED MAKEOVER:
FROM MS. INDEPENDENT TO
MS. FEARLESS

To stop being mistyped as Ms. Independent, you are going to have to change the way you feel about yourself and relationships. You have to start seeing yourself as the wonderful potential mate you are. Be assured that there is nothing about you that would make a man want to hurt or betray you. You can't continue to view dating relationships as battlegrounds where you always get wounded. All relationships have their ups and downs, but they do not inherently involve pain. Once you change your mind-set, you are going to have to take some risks. You need to date. And you need to test the waters to see who and what works for you and what doesn't. Eventually, changes in the way you think and behave will cause you to attract a different type of man, and going forward you will react very differently to his attempts to show you love and affection.

If you have been dissatisfied with your love life for a while now, you may be using your career or other projects as an escape—a way to avoid relationships. Now is the time to address these feelings, so you can slowly bring fun and romance back into your life. Try the following strategies:

Take a risk and date. The only way to prove to yourself that every relationship isn't doomed to failure is to go out there and have a great time dating. Of course, that won't be possible until you adjust some things, because you know how to sabotage relationships! You are too ready to blame a man, when sometimes the reason you get hurt is that you are acting up in the relationship. You are doing it to protect yourself, but that very protection can turn men off and drive them away. Being defensive, purposefully not returning phone calls or e-mails, and not returning affection (or pushing his affection away) are all things that can turn away a man who is interested in you. You know what a brush-off is, and you know when you do it. Stop doing it out of fear, and allow yourself to enjoy other people. I know it is a risk, but you will remain miserable until you try. You have so much more to gain than you have to lose.

Allow yourself to feel. When you finally allow yourself to date, after a reasonable amount of time you have to also allow yourself to be vulnerable—and then feel good about the experience. You have to allow yourself to enjoy dating and go with the flow. Stop trying to control your emotions. You'll only hold back feeling good if you are waiting for something bad to happen. Laugh, get butterflies in your stomach, and blush! As long as you are receiving signals that he is still interested, enjoy the fun of dating. You won't get the happy relationship you want if you are trying to date without allowing yourself to feel. You don't want to let go, because you feel you will fall. But you won't know that you're okay until you let go and land safely.

Stop looking for things to hide behind. Ms. Independent is good at finding ways to avoid relationships. In addition to becoming consumed with work, she will focus her time and energy on solving other people's problems, renovating her home, losing weight, and doing any other kind of project that can take over her life. Finding the right person isn't easy, and it requires time. As long as you use up all of your time doing other things, you won't have any time left for love. If this describes you, you may need to cut back on some of your activities in order to make new friends and date.

Acknowledge that all men are not the same. You may have dated so many "dogs" that you believe that all men are alike. Not all men are the same. The good guys are out there, although they can be hard to find. Sometimes women are looking in the wrong places, or they might be doing something to sabotage their ability to meet Mr. Right. Either way, just because you haven't found him yet doesn't mean that he doesn't exist. The point of this book is to help you realize the dating habits that get in the way of you finding Mr. Right. I've also shared with you the different types of Mr. Wrongs you are attracted to and who are attracted to you, so that you can avoid them and seek out a new type of mate. This information should make you feel confident that there are more good men out there. Now that you know who to avoid, and how to avoid them, you can increase your chances of finding someone good for you. It's time for you to stop assuming that all men are alike and give dating a good man a chance.

Face your past. When you stop to examine your dating history, it will help you better understand what went well, what didn't, and why. Sometimes we have to stop and think about what we've been through, in order to appreciate how strong we are and to remind ourselves that we can survive and overcome anything. When you look back over your relationships, try to understand what happened so that you can feel confident that you know how to address that situation better today than you did back then. Once you know what you need to change, you can have a more positive outlook on your dating future, realizing that your past does not have to dictate your future.

Develop confidence. Being hurt or betrayed by someone you cared about can have a negative impact on your self-esteem and confidence. If you have experienced a series of disappointments and you've lost the confidence you once had, now is the time to work on building it back up. How these men treated you in the past is a reflection of what's wrong with them, not an indication that something is wrong with you. However, you may not see it that way. You have to think positive thoughts about yourself and focus on all the things that make you great. This will help you develop or rebuild your confidence. When you become more confident, you will be less anxious and fearful because you will have more faith in your ability to choose appropriate mates, and to respond to any inappropriate behavior quickly and effectively.

Confront the negative voice within. One reason we continue feeling or acting badly is that a voice in our head keeps repeating the same negative messages over and over. If that voice is saying that you will never find love, that you aren't marriage material, or that men can't be trusted, how can you feel comfortable going out there and taking a risk? Tell that voice to shut up! Make a list of all the negative things it keeps saying, and really think about whether they are true. Where does the evidence really take you? I bet you'll be surprised. For each thing on the list, change the negative to a positive. Is it true that you aren't marriage material? Or is it that you haven't given yourself the time to meet anyone, let alone fall in love and get married? Is it true that all men can't be trusted? Or is it that you once dated someone with his own personal issues who could not be? Is the rest of the male race really like him? No. See what I mean? That voice in your head will lie to you, until you stand up to it and insist that it get a new and more positive attitude! (For more on this exercise, see the Ms. Typed Makeover Kit.)

Widen your social circle. In an attempt to avoid dating, sometimes Ms. Independent avoids everything else. If you have been avoiding going out and meeting new people, you should get out there and make some new acquaintances. Don't allow your exes to discourage you from being social and having a good time, for fear that the fun will eventually lead to disappointment. Go out, socialize, and even casually date. If you aren't ready to start dating yet, that's okay, but don't miss out on the fun that being social with women and men can offer you. You can hang out without giving or taking numbers or hooking up with someone. Whatever you do, don't become antisocial or a loner. You still want to enjoy friendships and social settings until you decide that you are ready to give dating another chance.

Be optimistic about your future. The pain and disappointment that men have caused you may have turned you into a pessimist. Instead of seeing the good in things, you may have become a "glass is half empty" person. Remember, if the glass is half empty, then it's also half full. You may be so frustrated with your love life that you lose confidence and enthusiasm about your life in general and expect that other things won't work out for you, just as you believe that dating never works out in your favor. Don't let your past sabotage your future. I know it's hard, but you have to maintain a positive outlook on dating and on your life. Being pessimistic is like letting the people who hurt you "win." Be optimistic about your future. Don't let anyone steal your joy!

10

Ms. Rose-Colored Glasses

WHAT SHE LOOKS LIKE

◆ Believes only the good things men say and ignores their bad habits and the warning signs that are signaling trouble. She talks too much and listens too little.

◆ Overlooks her man's flaws because she wrongfully assumes he is going to change. She patiently waits for a change that won't be coming.

◆ Doesn't understand that it's what he *does*, not what he *says* that matters most.

◆ Acts too optimistic. Her glass is always half full when it comes to dating, even if it's half full of poison.

♦ Has many other names including Ms. Denial, Ms. Can't Judge a Book by Its Cover, and Ms. I Don't Want to Hear it.

Ms. Rose-Colored Glasses won't see the truth about a man or what's wrong with their relationship. She just wants to be happy and see the best in her mate. Therefore she overlooks critical information about the men she's dating and ignores behaviors and events that should cause her to look at the relationship differently, if not end it. When men turn out not to be what she's looking for, she puts on her rose-colored glasses, sees what she wants, and ignores the rest. She denies the information she receives with all six senses so that she can believe what she wants about a man.

THE ROLES SHE PLAYS

There are several roles that Ms. Rose-Colored Glasses plays in relationships, including:

♦ **Ms. Can't Judge a Book by Its Cover.** When it comes to her man and their relationship, she ignores red flags, like his not introducing her to his friends or family, or not taking her to his job or home.

♦ **Ms. I Don't Want to Hear It.** She fails to ask questions, to get more background information on the man she's interested in, and to make sure her man is who and what he claims to be. She avoids information that might discourage her from moving forward. When a man tells her he is no good or that he doesn't do well in relationships, it goes in one ear and out the other.

◆ **Ms. Denial.** She pays more attention to what he says than to what he does. No matter how bad he treats her, as long as he tells her he loves her or wants to be with her, she ignores how he acts and focuses on what she wants to hear and believe.

> *Just Like You* ....
>
> *Who else is like Ms. Rose-Colored Glasses? She has a lot in common with Ms. Mom and Ms. Soul Mate. She is often very focused on doing whatever it takes to be in a relationship and make it work, even if it means ignoring important information. She will do anything to stay happy and comfortable in her situation. So if you are Ms. Rose-Colored Glasses, don't forget to read about Ms. Mom and Ms. Soul Mate.*

KRISTIN'S STORY

Kristin couldn't understand why Tyler was so reluctant to introduce her to his parents. They had been dating for almost a year, and she believed that if things were as serious as he said, then his parents should get to meet the woman he claimed he always talked to them about. Tyler shared that they had a soft spot for his ex-wife (with whom he had a daughter) and that in general they had very high expectations of all women, so he preferred not to introduce them to anyone he was dating.

It probably wouldn't have bothered her so much if he didn't still seem like such a mystery to her. She really wanted to know more about his life and what he was like outside their relationship. She had met only one friend of his who they bumped into on the street. She had never been to his job, and she knew his daughter from the picture that he carried in his wallet. The closest she had been to his house was waiting for him in the driveway with the car running, while he quickly ran inside for something he needed; she had never been inside. He said his place was too small and dirty and not even half as nice as hers, so why should they hang out there? That was fine with her because she had no desire to sleep or shower in a dirty bachelor pad.

One day she decided she wanted to meet his parents and would make it easy for him to pull everyone together. Earlier that week he had mentioned that he was going to a potluck dinner at their house on Thursday night after work. So she decided to surprise him at his job with a dessert in hand, hoping that that would inspire him to take her along. She went to his office building and had to ask a few people where he sat. When she finally met someone who knew Tyler, the woman said, "Oh, is that for tonight's potluck dinner? You just missed him and his wife, but you can follow me if you want."

Kristin still can't remember what happened to the cake she had been holding.

So What?

So we can't be mad at Kristin, right? After all, this man lied to her and obviously deceived her for months. Couldn't this have happened to anyone? Not necessarily. It wasn't Kristin's fault that it happened, but it would not happen to everyone. Kristin was not responsible for what Tyler did, but she did ignore a lot of red flags. Her gut told her that something was wrong, but she ignored it, whereas a different woman who trusted her intuition and instincts would not have let sign after sign go unaddressed. Something was wrong in her relationship with Tyler, yet she didn't ask questions or spend time getting to know him before they became intimate. She had only a cell phone number (he said he didn't have a house phone), she never met his family (he said they were anti-social), she never met his friends (he said they were always traveling for work), and she never spent time in his house (he said it was messy). The list went on.

Women can't go through relationships wearing rose-colored glasses, seeing only what they want to see and ignoring what they don't. They have to keep their antennae up and pay attention to all the information they are receiving so they can truly know what kind of person they are dealing with and whether he is worthy of their love. When you allow rose-colored glasses to color your vision, you lose focus on what you really need, by pretending you're getting what you're not. Be honest about what you want, and stay focused on what you need. Stop pretending that you already have what you need, or you'll never go out and get it.

Why It Matters

What are the negative consequences of being mistyped and seeing your your relationship with a man through rose-colored glasses?

You stay in an unhealthy relationship too long. When you aren't willing to be honest, you dress up unhealthy experiences in reasonable explanations. You call jealousy love, and you tell yourself your man was just kidding when he said he he drinks too much. You have to be strong enough to recognize and acknowledge when you are in an unhealthy relationship so that you can get out of it.

You put yourself in harm's way. While you are wearing those glasses, you could be missing lifesaving signals that are telling you to get away from the man you are dating. If you ignore or gloss over his controlling behavior or verbal abuse, more serious and potentially harmful experiences could be on the way. Ignoring these signs could cost you your health and, in the worst-case scenario, your life.

You feel angry and depressed. Many women become angry with themselves after the damage is done and they finally realize what they should have figured out long before. They feel depressed by the loss of the relationship and by the fact that they were so desperate to make the relationship work that they were willing to ignore almost anything to keep it.

You become distrustful. Even though you overlooked the truth, it's hard not to feel that your man intentionally misrepresented himself or deceived you. When you feel that most men say one thing and mean another, it's hard not to feel suspicious of men and carry that distrust into future relationships.

JUST HER TYPE

If you are Ms. Rose-Colored Glasses, given your tendency to put an overly positive spin on men and their behavior, you attract many of the undesirable types of men. You are especially vulnerable to men who want to be seen as nice men, not as the selfish manipulators they are. Each of the men below has a flaw that Ms. Rose-Colored Glasses will overlook. Be mindful of how vulnerable you are to each of these men and why:

Mr. Player. You are vulnerable to Mr. Player because, while wearing your rose-colored glasses, chasing him looks like so much fun. He comes off like the sexy bad boy that every woman wants, and when you are with him, you feel like a winner. Without the glasses, however, you can see that he is a user and that you are one of many women he is going to hurt before it's all over. It isn't possible to capture him or his heart, but from behind your glasses you can't tell.

Mr. Money. You are attracted to Mr. Money because he showers women with gifts and fine living. You are vulnerable to him because instead of seeing him as an egotistical man who uses his money to buy women's affection, you see him as a confident, generous man who loves to take care of his girl-friends by buying them expensive gifts.

Mr. Unhappily Married. You are vulnerable to him because instead of seeing that he wants to have his cake and eat it too, you feel sorry for him. You see someone who is unhappy and needs to be rescued from an unloving and unsupportive spouse. That is exactly what he wants—he wants you to be so focused on feeling sorry for him that you ignore the fact that he gets to have a wife and a girlfriend.

Mr. Pleasure Principle. You are vulnerable to him because he looks like a man who just can't get enough of your good sex, so you believe that you actually have a chance at a relationship with him. Reality check: he is interested only in having sex with as many women as possible. You have no chance of a relationship with him, and you aren't the only one who is giving him good sex.

Mr. Control Freak. You are vulnerable to Mr. Control Freak, because you interpret his behavior as expressing love and concern for you. Actually he's selfish and controlling. He calls you all the time to check on your whereabouts; instead of being disturbed, you think it's cute and a sign of how much he is into you. He's into you all right, but not in a good way.

Mr. Needy. He can make you feel so important that before you know it, he's got you hooked and is taking you for everything you've got. Instead of seeing him as the needy and selfish man he is, you see someone who wasn't loved enough and who needs to be nursed back to life with all of your undying love. You don't realize that his needs are so great that they will eventually smother and overwhelm you.

Mr. Under Construction. He has you fooled into thinking that he is on the verge of a huge breakthrough in all the important areas of his life. You think he is just about to finish school, get a great promotion at work, or move into a new apartment—the list goes on. What you don't know is that he has been "about to do" all of these things forever and somehow never does them. If you paid just a little more attention to what he does than to what he says, it would be obvious that his plans are nowhere near reality.

Mr. Abuser. He will have you thinking that his psychological and physical abuse is a result of his passionate and out-of-control feelings for you. His control will seem like a deep love and desire for more of you. Without the glasses, however, it is clear that this man is emotionally, spiritually, and physically harmful, and that any attempt at a relationship will result in you being injured.

Mr. Ex Factor. He can take advantage of you because you think he still has feelings for you and can't stop coming back for more. Actually he is your ex for a reason and wants nothing more than to be a friend with benefits.

Mr. Addict. Mr. Addict simply looks like a man who likes to party and have fun, but without the tinted lenses you're wearing, it is obvious he has a serious problem that requires professional help.

HOW YOU BECAME MISTYPED AS
MS. ROSE-COLORED GLASSES

Becoming Ms. Rose-Colored Glasses did not happen to you overnight. Chances are you first started learning her behavior as a child. You may have experienced many different events that influenced you, including:

- You learned from your family that it's better not to rock the boat by asking questions or examining situations closely.
- You were taught that it isn't your place to question what men say, and that you are simply supposed to take people at their word and at face value.
- Your mother was Ms. Rose-Colored Glasses in her relationships, and despite whatever drama she was experiencing, she chose to ignore her unhappy realities and press on.
- Your parents always felt that the glass was half full, and they taught you to see and interpret things that way, even if your first instincts were to recognize when something was wrong.
- As you were growing up, your friends wore rose-colored glasses, and you learned from them that there were certain things you were supposed to overlook in relationships.
- You dated a man who became very angry and upset when you asked questions, and his reaction taught you to fear asking men for more information.

- The discovery of unpleasant truths taught you to prefer to believe what men were presenting as the truth, rather than seek the truth out for yourself.

Let's not forget about how our culture influences us. It teaches women that every frog can be kissed and turned into a prince, and although logically speaking we know that isn't true, more than a few of us have unsuccessfully tried to smooch a froglike man into something we could tolerate. Now that you understand some of the different ways in which you became mistyped as Ms. Rose-Colored Glasses, going forward you can become more aware of how these influences are affecting you in your current relationships.

A Ms. Typed Makeover: From Ms. Rose-Colored Glasses to Ms. 20/20

If you have had enough of Ms. Rose-Colored Glasses, you will have to remember that facing the truth about yourself and your relationships can transform your life. The longer you live in denial about what is real, the longer it will take you to identify you true wants and needs, and the longer it will take you to pursue them. You won't accomplish your dreams if you convince yourself that what you already have is good enough. I know that facing the truth means you have to do something about what you discover, but don't be afraid to do it. Don't allow your fear to steal your joy. Now that you more fully understand what's been getting in your way, here are some suggestions that can help you move toward discovering your true dating personality:

Learn to read body language. You need to stop relying solely on what a man says while ignoring what he does. Suppose he ignores you or hasn't called in two weeks, and you finally track him down. When he says, "Come on, girl, you know I love you," don't believe it! Read between the lies and the lines. Forget about what he says—what's he doing? When his behavior and body language indicate a lack of interest, that should carry more weight than him filling your ears with meaningless words that don't translate into you being treated well.

Practice asking questions in a calm, relaxed, conversational way, but be sure to ask. There are probably lots of things you want to know about the man you are dating but are afraid to ask, so you may need to practice calm ways of asking questions. In a subtle way, he is under investigation, but you don't want to come across that way. You have to determine if this man is someone you should date. We already know you want to date him, which is what makes you throw on those rose-colored glasses so that you can only see what you want and ignore what you don't. But for your own health, take them off. Be willing to learn more about the man, and use that information to determine whether he is someone to casually date or someone with whom to be intimate.

Do your homework. You are entitled to know certain things about the man you are dating, especially if you plan to be intimate with him or be in a committed relationship with him.

Sometimes you equate asking questions with rocking the boat. Men who don't want to share their life will make you feel uncomfortable about asking questions. His unwillingness to share some basic information about himself is a sign to you to slow the relationship down. You should not be in a relationship with someone whom you feel you don't really know. When you make it clear that an open and honest dialogue about his life and lifestyle is what you want, you teach him exactly what you need and expect him to do.

It is reasonable to ask where he lives, where he works, what he does for a living and in his spare time, and if he has any children. I'm not saying to act like a prosecutor in court and interrogate him as the defendant. I'm saying that you better know who you are dealing with before you find out the hard way. You shouldn't have unprotected sex no matter what, but certainly if you take that risk, you should know if he has STDs or HIV. And it wouldn't hurt to have some indication about how he might react if you became pregnant. You have to think about these things ahead of time because some things can't be undone! Not that his past dictates his future, but it is a very good indicator, so knowing something about where he came from may tell you something about where the two of you are going. Use this information along with your current experience to determine if you should move forward with him, slow down, or stop.

Trust your intuition. Everyone has intuition and an inner voice that can help guide them through situations. If you learn to be still and notice what your inner voice is trying to tell you, you can follow your own best advice. Sometimes a thought will actually pop up and tell you what to do; other times a gut feeling will tell you that something is really right or really wrong. I'm sure you have heard stories where a person gets on an elevator (or bus or train—you name it) with someone and gets a funny feeling about that person or that situation, so they leave and then later learn that the person they saw later attacked someone else or did something horrible. We get vibes and gut feelings about people and situations all day every day, but the less you trust yourself, the weaker those messages are, and the quieter your inner voice becomes.

Learn to get quiet. Meditation or prayer will help you listen to your inner voice. Becoming more aware of your body and its natural sensations will help you notice when something within you is "talking" and alert you that you need to sit up and take notice.

Learn to recognize and acknowledge red flags. Whenever you look back on difficult situations, chances are that with hindsight you can see the warning signs and red flags that were there to make you aware. Pay attention to the information that rises to the top to inform you. You are not supposed to obsess over everything you see and hear, but you should notice when significant changes take place in a man's behavior, personality, or habits or in your overall relationship. For every type of relationship problem, usually some red flag lets you know something is wrong. A man's refusal to take you to his home is usually a red flag that he has something to hide. Not on the first date, but if you have been dating for weeks or months or are in a so-called relationship, seeing where he lives is only one of many things you would reasonably expect to know about him before reaching a certain level of intimacy or commitment. Maybe he lives at home with his mother or his wife, maybe his house is a pigsty, or maybe he doesn't want you showing up uninvited, but it isn't a coincidence that he won't take you there. His avoidance is a good example of a red flag. Some red flags you discover with experience, and others you can see just by paying attention to the lives of others. Your challenge is to open your eyes and question why things aren't as they should be.

Listen more than you talk. Sometimes you avoid seeing what's real by talking too much to hear what a man is trying to tell you. Women like to talk, and it's okay to talk, but you also have to listen to what men say. Men can tell you a lot about themselves in only a few words. When men tell you things like "I'm bad with money" or "I'm not the boyfriend type," don't dismiss it—believe them! If you're too busy cutting a man off when he's talking or changing the subject back to yourself, you will miss the important clues and information that you need to know to determine if you should date him or take the relationship to the next level.

Don't assume a man will change. When you're wearing your rose-colored glasses, you see potential in people that isn't always there. If your man needs a serious overhaul in many areas of his life, you shouldn't automatically assume that he is going to make the needed changes. Mr. Needy and Mr. Under Construction successfully win the dating game by convincing women that with a little help they can change, and only later do the women realize that the men had no intention of changing. At some point in our lives we've all been in a relationship where we really wanted to change something about our partners. Trying to change your man's basic personality or tendencies rarely works, though. That doesn't mean "once a cheater, always a cheater," but it does mean that whatever is inside a person that makes him feel the need to cheat over and over again can't be changed by a simple request to stop doing it, let alone by you overlooking it. If people change anything about themselves, it is because they choose to, not because you make them. This doesn't mean that you shouldn't ask; it just means that you have to be willing to accept the truth when asking isn't working. And it is up to you to change yourself because you can't change your man. You can't make your man stop being irresponsible or a jerk, but you can make yourself stop tolerating it.

Be confident in your ability to handle whatever comes your way. You often act like Ms. Rose-Colored Glasses because you feel you can't handle the truth. Instead you look through your glasses and see what you want to believe. When you develop the confidence to handle whatever comes your way, you can deal with hearing and knowing the truth about yourself and your relationship. That way you aren't looking to sugarcoat it—you take it and make a plan to deal with it. In the past, because you didn't want to deal with things, you looked the other way, but when you learn to accept that people and situations are flawed, you can focus on how to address those flaws instead of trying to avoid them. When you feel confident that you can handle whatever comes your way, you will take the glasses off.

Ms. Perfect

What She Looks Like

◆ Acts like a perfectionist in every area of her life.

◆ Tries to be perfect as a way of coping with her feelings of failure or unworthiness or a fear of rejection.

◆ Can't move her dating relationships forward as she is so caught up in meeting impossible standards.

◆ Has a chip on her shoulder and thinks that finding a man worth her time is unlikely. While dating, she looks for information to confirm how imperfect or inappropriate a man is for her.

- Finds herself alone because she is bored by, and has no patience for, men who aren't "good enough" for her. But her relationship success with "good enough" men isn't much better.

- Makes other people nervous because they know they are being judged, and they fear coming up short of her expectations.

- Doesn't know how to just relax and have fun, be silly, or live in the moment. She considers these things to be immature.

- Has many other names including Ms. As If!, Ms. Workaholic, Ms. Uptight, and Ms. Upward Bound.

Ms. Perfect is so caught up in the never-ending cycle of perfection and self-improvement that she has no time for a man. She is way too uptight to let go and have fun on a date, and she rarely finds a man who she thinks is "good enough" for her. Ms. Perfect spends her time and energy on perfecting herself, instead of living a balanced life that includes a relationship with a significant other. She focuses her energy on being good at everything, everything but having a loving romantic relationship.

THE ROLES SHE PLAYS

There are several other roles Ms. Perfect plays in dating relationships, including:

◆ **Ms. Judgmental:** She is so judgmental that she can't enjoy her life. She is always busy complaining about how no one and nothing is good enough for her.

◆ **Ms. Mogul:** She is the workaholic who doesn't have time or an interest in men who can't match her résumé. She is a professional Superwoman who stops only for Superman. Unfortunately for her, when she finally meets Superman, he doesn't think she's Superwoman!

◆ **Ms. Supermodel:** She is obsessed with beauty and isn't happy unless every hair on her head is in place. She looks red-carpet ready even if she is only headed to the mall.

◆ **Ms. Meticulous:** She insists that everything be in its place and look a particular way. She can't sleep at night with dishes in the sink; the cans in her cabinet have to line up with their labels facing out; and everything on her desk has an exact and proper place.

Just Like You ....
> Ms. Perfect's focus on fighting for perfection can sometimes make her similar to Ms. Drama Queen. Be sure to read about her too.

Ms. Typed

Karen's Story

Karen was a very successful and busy attorney. She never had time to meet men and was always looking for a mini-me. Her friend Janine felt she needed to set Karen up on a blind date. One time Janine hooked her up with Chris, who was equally successful, with a great personality and good looks. Janine knew that Karen had all the things a man was looking for, so they seemed like a good match. Their date started off slowly—he sat and watched her television for an hour. She was busy in her bedroom changing her outfit a half-dozen times. When she finally came out, she got upset when she noticed he was wearing shoes in her house. So with an attitude she said she was ready. And they were off to the movies.

Her wardrobe changes caused them to arrive late, so the movie she wanted to see was sold out. Karen complained about the movie theater and blamed them for not being more organized. She was so upset that she insisted they just leave. In an attempt to salvage the evening, Chris suggested they go grab a bite to eat. So they went to Karen's favorite restaurant, but there was a long wait for tables. She complained to the hostess that she was a regular, but there wasn't much that could be done. When seats finally opened up at the bar, she turned them down, but Chris was starving and suggested they take them anyway. Once at the bar, Karen went to the bathroom to text Janine to complain about Chris and their date.

When Karen returned, she was annoyed to discover that he had ordered them beers. She nastily told him she didn't drink beer. By then he had tolerated about as much of her attitude and nitpicking as he could. Meanwhile, since she wasn't seeing any evidence of the wonderful professional man Janine described, she decided to ask Chris some questions about himself. After about the fifth question, Chris excused himself to go to the restroom. Mentally he had checked out. When he returned, they sat in near-silence for the rest of the date as he watched sports on television and Karen sent angry text messages to Janine.

So What?

So what's wrong with Karen having such specific ideas about what she was looking for in a man and on a date? Shouldn't Chris have known to take off his shoes in her house? Wasn't it rude for him to order drinks without her?

Every woman should have some idea about what she wants and needs from a man so she can attract Mr. Right and repel Mr. Wrong. But if her requests are too specific and exact, she may never find the person she is looking for. He doesn't exist. And if her quest for perfection makes her a difficult person to deal with, chances are that even when she meets the man she is looking for, she is going to turn him off with her attitude and personality. That's what happened to Karen. She had a date with just the kind of man she said she wanted to meet, but the Ms. Perfect in her just wasn't ready to meet him and sabotaged it. She judged everything he did, and whenever things didn't go the way she planned, she reacted with a negative attitude.

Chris might have guessed to leave his shoes at the door because some people have that rule in their house, but he could just as easily have never thought of it. He never expected to come in, sit down, and stay for an hour, so why would he take off his shoes? And given how long it took to get a server's attention, Chris believed he was doing a good thing by ordering Karen a drink in advance. If she liked it, she could drink it, and if not, he would order her something else.

Karen had such specific expectations about how their date was supposed to go that when real life happened and things didn't go according to her plans, she couldn't recover and make the best of the situation. Everything had to be perfect. Chris's attempts to find a way to address her concerns and offer an alternative made her even angrier. She was offended that he would suggest she settle for anything less than what she wanted and felt she deserved. She was overly concerned with her appearance, where they went, where they sat, and what they drank. She couldn't appreciate or enjoy any part of their date because she was so unhappy with its failure by her standards. As much as she wanted things to be "perfect," it was never her intention to be mistyped as someone who was mean, judgmental, anxious, and unhappy all the time.

Why It Matters

If you are Ms. Perfect, what are the negative consequences when you allow perfection to dominate your love life?

You judge men harshly. The more of a perfectionist you are, the more you expect the man you are dating to be perfect. You expect the same level of success in career, education, and personal finances, when he may not be your equal in all these areas. Even when you claim to be okay with him not being your equal, he can tell that you're not. Sometimes it is obvious that he has not met your greater expectations of him, and he feels judged and lacking. Also when you are so judgmental, you usually jump to conclusions and use incomplete information to measure him and assess his situation. You can observe one small detail and rush to conclusions about him that the detail doesn't prove. It's yet another way that you miss out on the possibility of developing a new relationship.

You experience less pleasure and fun. When you are busy picking yourself and your date apart, it's hard to have a good time. Being overly concerned about doing it "perfectly" can take all the fun out of your date. You can't worry about every little thing. You have to learn to accept things as they are and have fun, even if your date or other circumstances aren't as ideal as you would have liked.

You avoid intimacy. It's hard to get close to someone if you are focused on what he looks like or how your lives look on paper. To really get to know a man, you need to see past his societal identity and see who and what he is inside. Not his clothes, his status, or his job—his soul. If you can't get past titles and credentials, you won't truly get close to anybody.

You fear being judged. The more you judge, the more you fear being judged, and the harder you work at being perfect. As long as you continue to be so hard on people, you will believe that they are looking at you with equally hard eyes, even if they are not. So you feel and act defensive with your dates. You are often surprised to discover that men don't hold you to nearly as high a standard as you hold them. But since you aren't sure, you always strive for perfection anyway. In this way, being mistyped as Ms. Perfect can be very stressful.

Just Her Type

If you are Ms. Perfect, you are attracted to men who you believe value perfection as much as you do. The expectation of a perfect man makes you vulnerable to:

Mr. Money. Mr. Money is in some ways a male version of you. He is very successful, holds himself to high standards, and deals only with the best. You are vulnerable to him because his perfectionism will bring yours out even more. He won't help you to relax and let go of some of your high expectations—just the opposite.

Mr. Unhappily Married. You enjoy men who are financially well off, successful, and powerful because they are close to your definition of perfect. You are vulnerable to him because he meets your criteria and you work so hard at being perfect that you feel confident that he would leave his wife for the opportunity to be with you. Of course your assumption is wrong. First, many men don't want to deal with the pressure and demands of a woman who thinks she is perfect. And second, his dating you doesn't suggest that he has any intention of leaving his wife, regardless of how perfect you are. Most women who date married men make the same false assumption that if they do everything he wants, he will leave. But usually he doesn't.

Mr. Control Freak. As if you weren't hard enough on yourself, Mr. Control Freak will demand even more from you. He has his own definition of perfection, and he will have you working hard to meet it. You are vulnerable to him because you have to meet both your expectations—and the resulting pressure and demands are overwhelming and unbearable. Ultimately you need someone who will accept you just the way you are, not someone who is trying to change and control you.

How You Became Mistyped as Ms. Perfect

You are probably wondering when and how you became Ms. Perfect. Chances are you have been in the process of becoming her for many years, probably since you were a young child. Some of the experiences that may have led you to become Ms. Perfect include:

◆ Your parents had very high standards, and you felt pressure to be successful and a high achiever, otherwise you would be criticized or punished.

◆ There were circumstances in your life that made you feel you needed to be the very best in order to be accepted or to make your family happy. If you had a sibling who was always in trouble or if someone in your family was very sick, you may have felt responsible for making up for those family problems by trying to be perfect and a source of pride for the family.

◆ Things were unstable at home, and trying to be perfect was your way of coping with those issues.

- You observed your dad or mom acting like Mr. or Ms. Perfect and learned from watching them that you should not rest until you achieved your goals, and once you achieved your goals, you should create bigger goals.
- Your friends were Ms. Perfects, and you looked up to them for it.
- You believe that you have to be perfect to attract and keep a man. You believe that being anything less than perfect makes you vulnerable to rejection or a breakup.
- You dated men with very high expectations of you who made you feel bad when you made mistakes or didn't meet their expectations.

Our society exerts a lot of pressure on women to do it all. In a struggle that many women face daily, they are expected to be great daughters, mothers, wives, friends, coworkers, and confidantes, and the list goes on. They can't find the time to be successful at work and also be the kind of wives and mothers they want, but they are expected to do it, no matter what the cost. This belief has led many women to seek perfection while also becoming angry, anxious, and depressed in their attempts to achieve it at all times. Having high standards can be a very positive motivator. It becomes a problem when you don't meet your expectations and punish yourself or get criticized by others. Seeking perfection can ruin your enjoyment of your life. And few people are there to tell you it's okay to do your best, to be excellent at some things but only good or average at others. Women walk around with tremendous guilt about not spending enough time with their children and then resentment for not spending the necessary time to excel at work. Women are caught in a bind.

To cope with all these different influences, you may need professional help. It will also require you to stop measuring yourself against anyone else's yardstick and learn to make decisions that work for and benefit *you* and *your* family. What works for another woman has nothing to do with what might work for you.

A Ms. Typed Makeover: From Ms. Perfect to Ms. Perfectly Satisfied

If you are ready to say goodbye to being mistyped as Ms. Perfect, you can start by releasing the pressure and responsibility of being perfect in all areas of your life, especially in romance. The more unrealistic your expectations, the greater the likelihood you will disappoint yourself, and you will find your date a disappointment. Here are some suggestions to help you move away from Ms. Perfect:

Don't be so hard on yourself. As Ms. Perfect, you see your life and behavior as either a success or a failure, with nothing in between. It's one thing to strive to be the best, but it's another to be unhappy with anything less than the best. Since you have such high standards, far too many things miss your mark for success and fall into the failure category. They aren't truly failures, but because your standards are so high, you feel and react as if they were. As a result, you feel angry, disappointed,

211

and sad. You are so hard on yourself that when you don't reach your intended level of success, you get really down and beat yourself up. This accomplishes nothing more than making you feel bad and puts even more pressure on you to perform at an even higher level next time. The more you repeat this cycle, the more you will exhaust yourself. You will be left feeling anxious and unhappy most of the time, living in fear and anticipation of possible failure.

Stop looking for mini-me. Many Ms. Perfects assume that their ideal mate is a mini version of themselves. You can want a man who shares your values and beliefs, but that doesn't mean he has to be an exact replica of you. You don't need matching bank accounts, degrees, cars, or designer brands. Your ideal mate shouldn't be you; he should complement you. Don't get so caught up in thinking that everything you've accomplished is the one and only best thing to have. Someone else can still be a good match for you, even if he hasn't copied your every move. There isn't one right way to do most things; instead there are several good ways. There is no best school or best company—many have good things to offer. And the same goes for men. There isn't just one who has all the right things. Some have a lot of one thing and a little of something else. You get to decide which combination is best for you.

Don't take on other people's responsibilities. Being Ms. Perfect puts so much pressure on you that you take responsibility for everything that happens around you. You have somehow convinced yourself that you can control what you do and the people in your life. You are already overburdened by your own responsibilities. You can't afford to hold yourself responsible for everyone else's too. If it isn't up to you to do it, then you need to let it go.

Blow off some steam. The pressure to be perfect can be overwhelming and exhausting. You need to learn how to relax at the end of the day, and especially at the end of a big project or a prolonged stressful time. Try exercise, yoga, meditation, prayer, massage, or a bubble bath. Find a hobby, and make it a regular part of your life. If all you do is work, work, work, you will stay stressed. You may enjoy cooking, gardening, painting, shopping, or travel. Make a commitment to yourself to spend some time doing something to help you relax at least once a week. Work your way toward once a day.

Learn gratitude. Ms. Perfect could live a blessed life full of love and wonderful experiences, but even then she would raise her expectations higher so that she couldn't appreciate what she did receive and accomplish. Take time out to count your blessings and acknowledge your successes. As much as you expect and demand the best, you will not always receive or experience it, so you have to learn to be thankful for all the great things you have. Shift your point of view from what you don't have to what you do. Whether you keep a gratitude journal or you count your blessings each day before you go to bed, you need to make a habit of acknowledging all the positive things, people, and experiences in your life. Express your gratitude for those things and you will start feeling more positively about your life.

Lose the fantasy. There is absolutely nothing wrong with having high aspirations and wanting the best. The problem comes when you can't enjoy what you have or how much you've accomplished. As a perfectionist, you may have such a specific idea of what you want in a man and in your life together that you make it very difficult to find something real. There are no relationships where two people don't ever disagree. A lot of women fantasize about a man who is a superstar multimillionaire who also spends a lot of time at home with his wife and kids just hanging out. Those two things don't go together. A millionaire has to spend a lot of his time working and is frequently away from his family and home. But that doesn't stop women from fantasizing that they are going to get the best of everything. I'm not saying don't strive for it, I'm just saying don't make it your one and only desire. Be willing to discover that another option might be good or better than your original idea.

Put yourself in his shoes. If you stop and put yourself in your man's shoes, you may start to appreciate the impact your perfectionism has on the people around you. Walk yourself through a day in his life, paying attention to how you usually interact with him. How much of what you say and do is judgmental? How many unrealistic expectations and demands do you place on him? How many times do you overreact to situations and cause a scene, or make a big problem out of something small that should be easily worked out? Once you begin to see a pattern in your behavior, you can create a list of things to do differently going forward.

Manage your expectations. As if you aren't stressed enough, you tend to see the glass as half empty. You anticipate other people not living up to your expectations, but not everything is as bad as you make it out to be. You waste energy worrying about how men might screw things up. Try to be more realistic. Most times things are fine, even when they aren't done to your high standards. People are not perfect (yourself included), so the more you sit around worrying about those imperfections, the more miserable you will be. You can't control others. The more you try, the unhappier both of you become. This is the time to learn to accept people as they are, yourself included.

Get professional help. If being Ms. Perfect is a result of some very difficult or traumatic past experiences, you may consider getting some help from a mental health professional. Sometimes even when we understand intellectually what we need to do differently, it's still hard to make change happen alone. Perfectionism can be connected to deeper psychological issues, so you may want to partner with someone to help. Once you deal with the feelings that are fueling your perfectionism, you will be happier.

Transform your thinking. Changing how you behave starts with changing how you think. You have to stop thinking in terms of absolute failure or success and be open to more than one way of living and being. Your view of your life is slanted. You see problems where they don't exist, or you believe that small issues are really big ones. Start this transformation by digging deep and trying to understand yourself first. Start by recognizing your negative beliefs about yourself, your life, and those around you. Then stop and question those beliefs. Is what you think about yourself and others a true and fair assessment? Create new, healthier, more honest, and more accurate beliefs about yourself and your life. (See the Ms. Typed Making Kit for more information.) Your actions will follow your thoughts. When you stop judging and start accepting, your life will change. That change will bring a different type of man and new kinds of dating experiences into your life.

Celebrate what is great about you, and accept what is not. For too long you have viewed yourself as not good enough: not pretty enough, smart enough, sexy enough, thin enough, or accomplished enough. Now is the time to step back and take a truly objective inventory of yourself and your life. Give yourself credit for how great you are and how much you have accomplished in life. The goal of being perfect causes you to strive to do too much, when if you already accepted and loved yourself enough, you could stop your quest. It is very hard to find love when you are so hard on yourself and everyone else around you. If you don't feel lovable, that makes it difficult for you to love or to accept love. Start by lovingly accepting who you are. If you don't love yourself first, how can you expect men to love you?

You may be a work in progress, but that doesn't have to stop you from celebrating how far you have come! Everyone can think of something they'd like to change about themselves, but the happiest and most successful people don't go around focusing on their flaws all the time. Doing so gets in the way of living. If you want to be happy and have a strong dating relationship, you are going to have to throw away the microscope that you are living under and start living.

The Ms. Typed Makeover Kit

Now that you understand your dating type and how you've become mistyped, I'm hoping you are hungry for more and ready to get started making some changes in your life. As much as we blame men for the pain in our lives and our failed relationships, we have to be honest about what we can do differently to change our experiences.

Don't beat yourself up about your type—you've been mistyped. Until now you have been reacting to what has happened to you, but now that you are aware of how your experiences have affected you, you can work on changing your life and rewriting your romantic future. This time when life happens, you won't let difficult times change who you are and what you believe about yourself.

In this section I have created exercises you can complete

to help you with your transformation. Many of these exercises focus on the whole of your life—that's because being healthy and well balanced is the best foundation upon which to build healthy dating relationships. First, I'll show you how to prepare the "soil" for the new you; then we'll walk through steps to plant seeds of change and allow those seeds to take root. As I mentioned earlier, I have completed all of these exercises myself and I refer back to them when I start feeling less like myself or that my focus is off.

There are three steps to your Ms. Typed makeover:

1. Create a vision for your life.
2. Let go of what's holding you back.
3. Take action.

I want you to spend some time thinking about what you really want out of life. You have been pondering what isn't working. Now I want you to focus on what you can do about it. This is your chance to dream big. During these exercises I want you to identify all of the thoughts and behaviors that are keeping you from achieving your goals and being your best self. We have already covered a lot of what may have been sabotaging your love life, so this is a chance to dig deeper to reveal any obstacles that might be keeping you mistyped.

After you create a wonderful plan, it is important that you make a commitment to just do it. When you put this book down, I want you to go out and live your best life.

Buy a journal or notebook that you can use to write down your thoughts on important life issues and questions. Your journal can be a simple notebook, or you can buy one that has a design or a message that inspires you. (Years ago, when I was living in Connecticut and dreaming of a life in New York City, I bought a journal with photographs of New York on the front and back to inspire and remind me of my dreams. Nearly a year later I started a job in New York!)

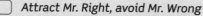

Check It Out: The Ms. Typed Makeover Checklist

Before getting started:

- [ ] Create a support team
- [ ] Give your home a makeover

Step 1: Create a vision for your life

- [ ] Imagine your Dream Life
- [ ] Take your Dream Life Inventory
- [ ] Become your own dating coach

Step 2: Let go of what's holding you back

- [ ] Make a list
- [ ] Face your fears
- [ ] Get closure

Step 3: Take action

- [ ] Attract Mr. Right, avoid Mr. Wrong
- [ ] Create a Dream Life Action Plan
- [ ] Pamper yourself

CREATE A SUPPORT TEAM

Let's face it, when you're going through hard times, your friends can make a huge difference in your ability to cope. A friend can be a patient listener with a shoulder to lean on, or a judgmental finger pointer who believes misery loves company and therefore gives terrible advice. If you are ready to make some important and positive changes, you will need supportive and positive people around you. These are the people you will call when you are struggling with a new challenge, doubting yourself, or slipping back into your type's old habits, or when you just want to get together for some girl talk and fun.

Who can you depend on to be supportive and encouraging during this time? Don't include anyone who might sabotage your success. And please, no friends who aren't ready to face their dating types themselves—they may be dealing with even greater challenges than you. Although we love them, sometimes our friends give the worst advice because they don't have their own heads, hearts, and lives in order. So don't blame a friend for steering you down the wrong road if you know she is the wrong person with whom to talk about these things.

Identify one to three people you feel can be supportive during this time. Talk to them and explain the challenges you are facing, and tell them how much you'd appreciate it if they were to support you.

My team:

1. _____

2. _____

3. _____

Give Your Home a Makeover

One of the things you can do to kick off your plan to change your love life is a home makeover. Take the time here to consider what in your environment at home, work, or school might be keeping you locked into your dating type, or what might be discouraging or distracting you from making the changes you desire. Then get rid of it! Examples of distractions include old photos, music that reminds you of the last man you dated, alcohol, or even certain "comfort" foods. For example, if you are trying to transform from Ms. Sex Machine, you might want to get rid of the things around your home that make you or your date immediately think about sex or that encourage you to jump into the sack sooner than you should. Be very open-minded, and look for the symbols, personal items, books, mementos, or other things that make you feel stuck in old habits that you want to break or that remind you of the unhappier times in your life that led you to become mistyped in the first place. Whatever you find, toss it or pack it up in a box. Store it somewhere out of sight and out of mind. If you have to, give it to someone else to hold on to, but don't have anything around you that will distract you or encourage you to fall back into your type's old habits. If Mr. Wrongs are still hanging around you trying to pull you back into your old life, erase their numbers from your cell phone. Put away those old photos and love letters. Clear a space for the new you!

Distractions to remove from my space:

1. _____

2. _____

3. _____

4. _____

5. _____

In addition to eliminating certain things from your environment, I want you to make a shopping list of things that will make your environment more supportive of your desired changes. This list could include adding things like artwork, new music, scented candles, fresh flowers—you name it. Make the list here or on a piece of paper in your journal. Then get out there and pick up what you need. I want the places where you live and work to be as comfortable, positive, and supportive as possible. I want you to feel encouraged and inspired in your personal space. Add things that represent the woman you strive to be.

Inspirational things to add to my space:

1. _____

2. _____

3. _____

4. _____

5. _____

IMAGINE YOUR DREAM LIFE

Imagine if you never stopped to think about what you wanted out of life. Obviously you would get something but nothing nearly as awesome as you could achieve if you took the time to examine your life and develop a plan for accomplishing what you want. Many people settle for whatever comes their way. Those people get mediocre results, though, because they have mediocre expectations. I know you are tired of accepting what comes your way by chance, especially when it comes to love—otherwise you wouldn't be reading this book. You can have the relationship you want, but you have to design and create it, first in your mind and then in reality. But you can't expect to be able to create something you can't even imagine. As the saying goes, people rarely achieve what they never thought was possible.

Now it's time to put a stake in the ground. Stop and think about what you really want out of life. What do you want for yourself personally and professionally? If you won't take the time to think about what you want and how to make it happen, then you can't be serious about wanting to change your life. Dreaming up the good stuff is the easiest part, so let your mind go and experience the fun of imagining your ideal life.

Imagine what your life would look like if you were currently living your best life. It doesn't matter if it is one year or ten years away—just imagine your ideal life. For the purpose of this exercise, assume that you are in a relationship with a significant other. You need to imagine the best life you could live with your partner. If you are trying to be the best person and best partner you can, you need to think about what things you would do to hold up your end of the bargain.

This exercise will help you imagine broader dreams for yourself—dreams to inspire you and move you forward, add meaning to your everyday life, and give it some long-term purpose. Keep in mind that at different times in your life the definition of your Dream Life is different, but ideally the core goals and desires are usually the same: security, a job that satisfies you, a healthy body and mind, and a relationship that is supportive and loving.

Don't worry about what you wanted in the past, what the old mistyped you would want, or what you think you're supposed to want. Just be honest with yourself about what the new you wants today. You can always change your mind later, but you have to start somewhere now. For the purpose of this exercise, imagine that you have already made certain positive changes to yourself and your life based on your type. Dream about your life as if you were not held back by any challenges from the past.

Answer these questions in as much detail as you can. It's okay to think about it for a while and to change your answers if needed. You may not have specific answers to everything, but you want to at least develop a general idea of your goals for each major area of your life. Write as much as you can—don't limit yourself.

In My Dream Life ....

RELATIONSHIPS

◆ **Romance.** Describe your relationship with your life partner. What are some of his qualities? What kind of things do you do together? What are your goals and aspirations as a couple?

....

....

....

◆ **Family.** How is your family life? What kind of relationships do you have with your family members?

....

....

....

◆ **Friendship/Community.** What kinds of people are your friends? Who are they? What kind of community do you live in? Do you belong to any community groups or social groups? If so, what groups, and what is your role?

....

....

....

MIND, BODY, AND SPIRIT

◆ **Health, Fitness, and Recreation.** How is your health? What do you do to stay physically fit? What do you do for fun? Describe any hobbies you have and how often you enjoy them.

....

....

....

In My Dream Life (continued)

• **Psychological Well-Being.** How is your mental health? Describe your general mood most of the time. When necessary, what do you do to manage stress, anxiety, anger, or sadness?

....

....

....

• **Spirituality.** What do you do for spiritual development and growth? Do you attend religious services? Do you do other activities like read, pray, or meditate?

....

....

....

• **Environment.** Describe your home. Are you in the city or country? What is your neighborhood like? Do you live someplace with a view of the ocean, mountains, or skyscrapers? Are arts and cultural opportunities nearby?

....

....

....

PROFESSIONAL DEVELOPMENT

• **Education and Personal Development.** Are you in school, or have you completed a certain degree? If so, what degree, and in what subject/discipline?

....

....

....

◆ **Career.** *If you are working, what is your career like? What do you do for a living and in what kind of place? Describe the kind of people you work with and what kind of work you do. Do you have a special title or role/responsibility at your job? Do you manage a staff, work in a team, or work alone?*

....

....

....

◆ **Finances.** *What is your ideal income? Do you have any investments or savings? Do you have any businesses or additional sources of income? Are you financially independent, or do you share your financial responsibilities with someone?*

....

....

....

Carefully review what you've written, and think about what your Dream Life is telling you about yourself. In my Dream Life I kept thinking about the media even though I was not yet involved in any way. I finally admitted my desire to work on television and write books. As much as I was afraid to try it and fail, my desire for it was so great that I had to stop denying it and just go for it! The same applies to you.

Think about what you've written and what you are trying to avoid. Then just embrace it. If you keep seeing certain words like *independence, health,* or *debt* (just as examples), those words are telling you something important. Don't ignore what you value and what you need to add to your life.

Now that you have started to identify what you want and you understand your type, you can make sure that your old habits don't sabotage your future. You should keep your Dream Life in mind as you make personal and professional decisions. Move toward the people and opportunities that are going to make your dreams come true, and move away from the men and situations that don't fit your plans.

Your Dream Life Inventory

Your next step is to figure out some strategies for accomplishing those goals. You didn't think we were just going to dream and not take action! This exercise is designed to help you make the Dream Life you just described a reality. For each area of your life write down where you are today, your future goal, and what steps you are going to take to reach that goal. In the last exercise you wrote about your Dream Life. Now you have to take inventory and determine how close or far away you are from your dream. For example, if in your Dream Life you want to become a lawyer, you could start by writing that you have a college degree today and that getting a law degree is your future goal, and then list the next steps you are going to take to get there, including taking the LSAT, researching law schools, talking to other lawyers about their careers, and so on.

Your Dream Life Inventory

Area of Your Life	Where You Are Today	Your Future Goal	Next Steps
RELATIONSHIPS			
Romance			
Family			
Friendship/Community			
MIND, BODY, AND SPIRIT			
Health, Fitness, and Recreation			
Psychological Well-Being			
Spirituality			
Environment			
PROFESSIONAL DEVELOPMENT			
Education and Personal Development			
Career			
Finances			

Become Your Own Dating Coach

Given how much you have learned about your dating type throughout the book, once you finish your Dream Life Inventory, you should focus on personal and relationship goals based on your dating type. You can start by creating a list of behaviors you need to change. Then write the goal you want to accomplish in addressing this behavior. For example, Ms. Anaconda might say that she wants to call her boyfriend less often. Her goal might be to avoid calling more than once every three hours. You should complete this list for each of your dating types.

TYPE:	
Behavior to Change	**Goal**

List What's Holding You Back

Take time to investigate how your dating type is negatively affecting your thoughts and feelings about yourself. It's those thoughts and feelings that caused you to become Ms. Typed in the first place, and now that you have picked up her bad habits, those habits are what keep this cycle going. You can't change what you don't acknowledge, so this is your chance to get it all out in the open. Address how you think and what you believe, so that you can work on changing those false or unhealthy thoughts and beliefs into truthful and positive ones.

Women often have beliefs about themselves that they do not realize lower their self-esteem, sabotage their success, and lead them to become mistyped. Maybe deep down you feel unattractive, so you ask yourself why a man would want to marry you. Whatever thoughts you have that might be holding you back need to come to the surface today. You need to expose them for the lies they are, and then eliminate them. List five thoughts that you believe are holding you back from the success you deserve in love and life. After each negative thought I want you to assume that that thought is a lie about you and write a more accurate positive statement. For example, Ms. Second Place's negative thought might be that she doesn't deserve to be first in a man's life. She could rewrite that as a positive statement by saying she is a wonderful woman who deserves to be first in her man's life.

Old Negative Thoughts That Represent Ms. Typed	New Positive Thoughts That Represent the True You

FACE YOUR FEARS

Fear is one of the most powerful emotions affecting our dating relationships. It influences how we act on dates, who we date, when we commit, what we tolerate, and so much more. Get in touch with how your fears may be holding you back and keeping you mistyped by writing down all the things you fear in relationships. Some of us fear we will be left alone; others fear exposing our true selves or our past mistakes. List the top five things you fear in relationships. What worst-case scenario are you always worrying about?

1. _____
2. _____
3. _____
4. _____
5. _____

Now that you have completed this exercise and come face to face with some of the fears, you may realize that the Dream Life you created isn't accurate, as you were holding back when you wrote it. Many of my clients have to redo it when they realize that they wrote what they thought would probably happen instead of writing what they *want* to happen. So many times we are afraid to say what we want. We don't want to ask for it and then fail to obtain it. Some people would prefer never to pursue a dream than to face this fear of failure. Take another look at your Dream Life, and make sure you didn't leave anything out because of fears or negative thinking about your abilities. This is your chance to plan out the life you want, so don't edit yourself. Don't let fear steal your dreams!

GET CLOSURE

Sometimes we carry around so much anger toward someone that even after the relationship is over, we don't have closure. The feelings are still there, just beneath the surface, affecting our thoughts about ourselves and influencing how we behave in our new relationships. One way to get closure is to write down your feelings.

Knowing what you now know, you may feel even more frustrated with the people who played a role in helping you become Ms. Typed or who took advantage of you. Letter writing is a way to express your feelings toward those people without having to confront them directly. You can identify someone from your distant or more recent past who you feel has caused you emotional harm or made things unnecessarily difficult for you, and write that person a letter. Get it off your chest, and say how you really feel without worrying about how the other person is going to react. Instead of having a funky screaming match with the person you want to confront, you are going to write all the things you wish you had said before or all the things you ever wanted to say but didn't. It is your chance to be heard without interruption and get graphic about exactly how you felt about your interactions with that person. This letter is going to help you bring your feelings to the surface, so that you can process them, then leave them behind you.

Write as many letters to as many people as you want. The letters should be long enough to say everything you need. There is absolutely no limit: five, ten, twenty pages—go for it. Don't leave out anything important, because when you are finished writing, I want you to feel relieved of the burden of carrying around all those feelings inside you. You can either seal the letters in an envelope and put them away in a box in your closet, or you can destroy them. Rip them to shreds or burn them. With this act of closure you'll be leaving your past and moving forward toward a clear, bright, baggage-free future.

MS. TYPED

ATTRACT MR. RIGHT, AVOID MR. WRONG

I shared with you earlier a description of the types of men you need to avoid and some things to look out for when dating. Dating the men to whom your current type is attracted is an obstacle to your changing and finding happiness with your true dating personality. Now it's time for you to make a personal list of men's characteristics that keep you mistyped and bring out the Ms. "_____" in you. These are the Mr. Wrongs you need to continue to avoid. Write down the characteristics and qualities you now know you need in a partner. These are the Mr. Rights that you want to attract and pursue. Refer back to this list as you meet new potential dates, and use it to help determine if you're staying on track.

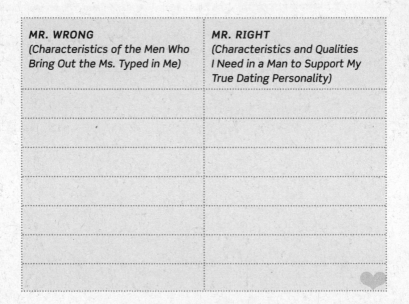

MR. WRONG (Characteristics of the Men Who Bring Out the Ms. Typed in Me)	MR. RIGHT (Characteristics and Qualities I Need in a Man to Support My True Dating Personality)

CREATE A DREAM LIFE ACTION PLAN

Now it is time to revisit the goals you set in your Dream Life and make a serious commitment to achieving them. Create deadlines. That's right—you need to build in some accountability. You can't say you are going back to school but never say when. For each goal that you listed in your Dream Life Inventory, you need to list a date or a timeframe by which you expect to complete your goal. For example, you can say March 31, end of the first quarter, or end of the year, but you need to put a deadline to your goal so you have a date to work toward. If your goal is a regular or ongoing activity, like going to the gym, you can write something like "daily" or "twice a week."

Dream Life Action Plan

Area of Your Life	Where You Are Today	Your Future Goal	Next Steps	Deadline/ Date
RELATIONSHIPS				
Romance				
Family				
Friendship/Community				
MIND, BODY, AND SPIRIT				
Health, Fitness, and Recreation				
Psychological Well-Being				
Spirituality				
Environment				
PROFESSIONAL DEVELOPMENT				
Education and Personal Development				
Career				
Finances				

Pamper Yourself

Positive change can be both an internal and an external experience. Much of what we have been focusing on is internal or emotional. But what you and others express on the outside can have a big impact on your dating and life experiences. If you feel it's time for a bit of change, why not try a fresh new look to celebrate the new you? You don't have to do anything drastic—it's really up to you. If you are ready for a big change, you can do something like cut or color your hair. But if you are looking for only a small boost, you can try a new outfit or change the color of your lip gloss. These things sound small, but for some women they can make a significant difference. The idea here is not for you to change who you are but to make sure that how you look on the outside is an accurate reflection of who you are and how you feel inside. You could be mistyped on the inside and the outside. You might be making big changes in your life but still look like the old you. If you want to remind yourself and let others know about the new you, you should look the part.

Don't be afraid to visit the makeup counter and ask for a new look. Many major department stores have free personal shopping services that can help you shop and find a new look for your wardrobe. We all have clothes in our closets that we were bold enough to buy but have not been confident enough to wear—own it, and wear it. I bet your gym offers sessions to meet with a personal trainer who can advise you on transforming your body to your ideal figure. What is it you'd like to change that you know would make you feel great? Pick something, and make at least one change that captures and reflects how good you feel about the new you.

One Last Thought

Through the years I've seen many smart women recognize what they're doing to hurt themselves and have a tough time trying to improve and change their lives. Their biggest challenge can be staying inspired or motivated to make a change.

We feel tired or overwhelmed, or that no one cares. Or we're convinced that no matter how hard we try to change, it won't make a difference. Sometimes we just need a pep talk. We need to hear what we already really know, to remind us how wise we are. It is powerful knowing that someone cares enough to hold us accountable for transforming our lives, for transforming our thoughts and actions in a way that will allow us to live well and to our best abilities.

That is why I wrote this book.

Hopefully, as you read through the chapters, you recognized yourself right away and immediately remembered all the times you allowed these issues to sabotage your love life, even though you knew you needed to do something about it. What's different this time is that we are here together, and I have provided you with the guidance and support to help you make long-lasting change. If you didn't have some idea already (which I doubt), you now know what you're doing to undermine your happiness and what you can do to stop it. This book was meant to be a catalyst for change and to get your creative juices flowing. No one can change overnight, but now that you know what you know, there's no turning back!

As a result of being mistyped, you may have forgotten how amazing you are. You have always had the power and ability to become any type of woman you want. The advice I provided here can only support that evolution. You might want to pursue a major dating type overhaul, or you may discover that you only need a few small tweaks to kick Ms. Typed to the curb. Either way, you are already on a path to positive change. Whether you realize it or not, reading this book has changed you already. It has changed the way you think and the way you see yourself. I hope that your new thoughts inspire you to try new things.

I wrote about these dating experiences because I see them in my clients, friends, and family members and in myself. We all struggle, and often unnecessarily. Sometimes we need inspiration or someone to give us a reality check and remind us how wonderful we are. Suffering through pain, loneliness, and disappointment is not supposed to be a daily part of your love life.

I am here to remind you how powerful and incredible you are, even when you don't feel that way. I hope that by showing you your dating type and exploring the past experiences that mistyped you, you will understand why you don't always feel as good as you should, and you will feel empowered to change. I know you can do it. And even though I am not there with you in person, I am there in spirit, cheering you on and encouraging you to keep going. Whatever you do, don't stop! This is a lifelong journey, and as long as you're here, keep on giving it your best effort.

Additional Resources

If you have been struggling with relationships or with getting your emotions under control for a long time, it could be a sign you should seek professional help. Even if you think things aren't that bad, but they aren't really that good either, you may want to work with someone to help you sort things out. There are several kinds of professionals you can see, including psychologists, counselors, social workers, or professional coaches. Below are some websites you can visit to learn more. They'll inform you about when to seek help and which type of professional to contact:

The American Psychological Association
www.apa.org

The National Association of Social Workers
www.socialworkers.org

The American Association of Marriage and
Family Therapy
www.aamft.org

The International Coach Federation
www.coachfederation.org

Acknowledgments

This book is a lifelong dream for me and it would not have been possible without the help of many important people who encouraged, inspired, and supported me both personally and professionally. Thank you to:

God for his unmerited favor and all of the blessings in my life. Words cannot properly express my gratitude for how God continues to transform me and my life.

My editor Heather Jackson and the entire team at the Crown Publishing Group. Heather saw the potential in me, and my ideas, and I knew when I met her and the Crown family I had found the right home for my book. She always encouraged me to listen to my own voice, and her extensive experience was valuable in shaping this manuscript. Heather and I share a vision for encouraging and helping women, and she provided very insightful feedback, suggestions, and advice throughout the writing process.

My literary agent Rebecca Oliver for her enthusiasm and commitment to this book from the moment we met. She helped me strengthen my proposal, fully flesh out new ideas, and find the perfect editor and publisher. I also want to thank Richard Abate for his comments on my proposal and for his insight to pair me up with Becka.

My agents at Endeavor: Nancy Josephson, Brittany Balbo, Ivo Fischer, Conan Smith, and Ruth Chen for their support and help with this book and my career.

Tyra Banks for extending her friendship to me and for inviting me to participate in many of her projects. I have learned a lot from our time together and I appreciate the opportunity.

Ricki Lake and the producers of *The Ricki Lake Show* for

giving me my "big break." I would also like to thank the producers at the *Today* show for being so supportive of my work over the years.

My family and friends, who have all supported my pursuit of education and my media career. In particular I would like to thank Garvin, Tyler, Mom, Walter, Ava, Adrienne, Netty, Dana, Jessica, Carl, Cindy, Angela, Kristin, Alison, and Mandell for your thoughtful and encouraging words along the way. So many have encouraged me to pursue the road less traveled, and I cannot tell you how grateful I am for your positive attitudes and your support tracing all the way back to the time when all of this seemed like a faraway dream.

My special "mothers" who have played such an integral role in my growth and development as a child and for all the years that we were here together: thank you, Anjanelle, Granny, Ann, and Mama Clyde. I hope you are celebrating in heaven when you see what we have done together.

My mother, Hawken School, Boston College, the University of Michigan, and Yale University for supporting my pursuit of higher education.

All of my teachers who supported my love for and pursuit of higher education. In particular I would like to thank Dr. A. Wade Boykin for encouraging me to pursue a doctorate in psychology and my doctoral dissertation committee at the University of Michigan: Dr. Toni Antonucci, Dr. Sandy Graham-Bermann, Dr. Richard Tolman, Dr. Vonnie McLoyd, and Dr. Leonard Eron.

Rev. A. R. Bernard, Pastor of Christian Cultural Center, for his invaluable spiritual teachings, guidance, and life coaching.

The countless women who I have coached and worked with in my research, private practice, and on television. You inspire me and keep me focused on my goals.

Anyone I have not named personally, but who has helped or encouraged me in this process: thank you. Thank you all for your support.

Index